Natural Sweets & Treats

Ruth Laughlin

Photographs by Brad Moulton
Illustrations by Richard Holdaway

LM
Publications

Mapleton, Utah

PREFACE

All my life I have had a sweet tooth. When I was a youngster, my father was a bee-keeper so we had plenty of honey to use, even during the depression. Sunday night candy pulls at our house were a tradition. We also preserved much of our fruit by drying. My inbred interest and experience in using both honey and dehydrated fruits are important facets of this book.

While in my late teens I was exposed to the world of natural foods and became intensely interested. I studied and learned of their value in bringing about and maintaining better health. More recently I learned the techniques of candy making from a professional candy maker. Knowing what I did about nutrition, I battled with my conscience over the use of so much white sugar, chocolate, etc. The solution was simple switch over to natural foods and use the same techniques.

For years I experimented, adapted, created, and compiled this material. I don't want to go on record as maintaining that even natural sweets are good for one in unlimited quantities. But since we are a sweet-oriented society, I decided to create and adapt recipes that would come as close to the natural 'as is practical.

It was a pleasant surprise to discover that these natural sweets are not only more nutritious but are better tasting and have marvelous eye appeal. In these recipes I am using natural sweets such as honey, dark brown sugar and molasses with fruits (dried and fresh), seeds, grains, nuts, carob, dry milk, whole wheat flour, etc. You will note that most of the ingredients are easily obtained from your grocery or local health food store.

At this time, with interest in nutrition at an all-time high, I am proud to make my contribution to "naturally" better eating.

RUTH LAUGHLIN – 1973

TABLE OF CONTENTS

INTRODUCTION

CAROB FOR CHOCOLATE

Carob is the little-known fruit of a tree originally cultivated along the Mediterranean. The long, dry pods of the carob tree contain hard seeds in a sweet pulp. Grind this fruit into a fine powder and you have a carob "flour." Taste it and you think you have chocolate.

By no means, though, should carob be classed only as a substitute food.

Carob has nutritional values that make chocolate look pale by comparison. It has as much thiamin as asparagus, strawberries, or dandelion greens. And carob has as much niacin as dates or lima beans. In riboflavin content, carob ranks with brown rice.

There's more vitamin A in carob than in equal amounts of eggplant, beets, raisins, onions. And carob contains good quantities of important minerals like calcium, phosphorus, iron, copper, and magnesium.

Carob's value as a health food is emphasized by its use as a remedy for diarrhea. It has a high pectin content. Pectin is a valuable food ingredient and offers natural protection against diarrhea.

Carob has none of the allergenic properties that chocolate has. It is much lower in calories and is not a stimulant.

It's most pleasing feature - tossing aside all the good for you qualities - is that it tastes like that old, everyday chocolate. Carob is available in all health food stores. It comes in chunks that can be melted and used like cooking chocolate and in flour form, a delicious substitute for cocoa.

In recipes calling for carob chips, carob coating can be cut in small bits.

COOKING WITH HONEY

Honey may be used, measure for measure, in place of the sugar in preparing puddings, custards, pie fillings, baked apples, candied and "sweet-sour" vegetables, salad dressings, and cinnamon toast. Brushed or drizzled on ham during the last half hour of baking, honey adds flavor and gives a golden glaze.

Cakes and cookies made from honey remain moist in storage. Some are improved in flavor and texture when aged a few days. Crisp cookies, however, are likely to lose crispness on standing. Some honey candies and frostings may stay too soft in humid weather. For cakes and cookies made with honey,

You'll get best results if you use recipes developed especially with honey as an ingredient.

Use mild-flavored honey for bland fishes. Honeys with stronger flavor may be used in spice cake, gingerbread, brownies, and in other rather highly flavored products. In any recipe, be sure to scrape all the honey out of the measure for accurate amounts. See page 115 for additional information on honey.

BAKING WITH WHOLE WHEAT FLOUR

Fine stone-ground flour is best in the recipes in this book from the standpoint of texture and flavor. No longer is enriched white flour accepted as an equal substitute for 100 percent whole wheat flour among nutritionists and other health-minded people.

There are people who prefer white flour baked goods; yet a taste for the full, rich flavor of whole wheat sweet breads, cakes, cookies, and pastries can be acquired, given half a chance. Once you get used to whole wheat baked goods, the white products are tasteless.

Young mothers would do well to start their children out on whole wheat sweets, thereby supplying them with much-needed nutrients for growth. Adults will be better able to maintain vigor and general good health by eating whole wheat products that supply vital vitamin B complex and vitamin E.

Some people worry about calories in whole wheat - of course there are calories, but you eat less of whole wheat goodies because of the feeling of satiety derived from them.

For those who prefer not to use soda and baking powder for leavening, low-sodium baking powder and other substitutes can be purchased at a health food store. Included in this book are several recipes that do not call for leavening.

EQUIVALENTS

1 stick or ¼ pound butter or margarine =½ cup

2¼ cups firmly packed brown sugar = 1 pound or 16 oz

1 cup chopped nuts = ¼ pound or 4 oz

1 tbsp. vinegar plus sweet milk to make 1 cup = 1 cup sour milk
(may be used in recipe that calls for buttermilk)

juice of 1 lemon = 3-4 tbsps.

grated peel of 1 lemon = 1 tsps.

juice of 1 orange = 6 to 8 tbsps.

grated peel of 1 orange = about 2 tsps.

12 to 14 egg yolks = 1 cup

8 to 10 egg whites = 1 cup

1 whole egg = 2 egg yolks

1 slice bread = ½ cup soft crumbs

12 Graham crackers = 1 cup fine crumbs

3 level tbsps. carob powder plus 2 tbsps. water = 1 square chocolate or:
replace 3 tbsps. flour per cup with 3 tbsps. carob powder

chopped carob bar or coating in small pieces = carob chips, if not available.

.

.

DRIED FRUIT, SEED
AND NUT CONFECTIONS

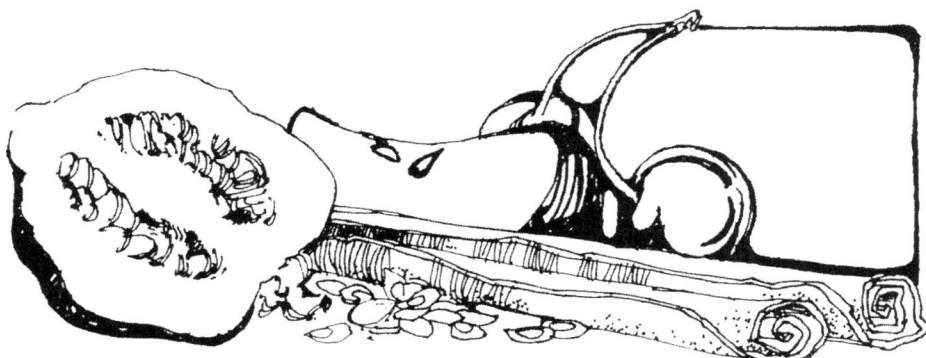

HOME FRUIT DEHYDRATION

To remove water from food, a combination of heat and warm, moving air is best. The faster the drying process, the more vitamin C is retained and the more natural color is maintained.

Heat from the sun is the most ancient method and is still widely used, especially in parts of the country where the sun is hot. A framed screen propped on supports with netting over the fruit works well. The screen can be; placed on the flat roof of a patio or garage. A fast method is to place old glass windows over the fruit to intensify the sun's rays.

The oven method is not too efficient, because the moisture and the temperature are difficult to control and air movement is nearly impossible. The oven door must be propped open a few inches to allow moisture to escape.

A specially built dehydrator is the best method. A heating element such as a heat cone (600 or 1000-watt light bulb in bottom of the cabinet) provides the heat. A fan directed on the heat cone circulates the hot air up through the racks. Two holes covered with screen on either side at the bottom of the cabinet provides air intake. A vent in the top allows the moisture to escape.

Cover the screened racks with nylon net for easier removal of dried fruit. Lightly oiling the screen helps too.

For more details and complete instructions on dehydrating plus a picture of a dehydrator, see the book *Passport to Survival* by Esther Dickey, or the updated version by her daughter Rita Bingham.

SYRUP FOR DEHYDRATING FRUITS

2 cups water
2 cups honey or 1½ cups sugar and
½ cup corn syrup. (For lighter syrup,
decrease honey to 1½ cups)

2 tsp. ascorbic acid powder (available in
markets near canning supplies) or juice
of one large lemon.

Combine ingredients and warm enough to mix together. Cool. Dip halved or sliced fruit in syrup and drain thoroughly before arranging on rack, cut sides up. This syrup helps to maintain good color and gives the fruit a good sweet - sour coating – makes it a real confection.

Fruits do not need to be dried completely before storing. When fruit is rubbery and there are no moist spots, it can be packed rather tightly in clean glass jars. Cover jars with clean lids and screw bands loosely. Set fruit into a pre-heated 200° F oven for 30 minutes. Remove jars from oven, tighten bands and cool. Fruit will be soft and pliable when ready to use.

If this method isn't practical, completely dry fruit and store in odd jars or cans. When ready to use, soften fruit by pouring water into the container, then draining it. Tighten lid and let stand a few hours.

FRUIT LEATHER

Best fruits for fruit leather:

Apricot	Any Berry	Apple
Peach	Pear	Apple and Pineapple
Nectarine	Prune	Bananas

Puree very ripe fruit in blender. Add honey, if you desire, to taste. Pour out very thin (¼ inch thick) on lightly oiled cookie sheets or pour out on plastic wrap that has been secured to cookie sheet with tape. This helps to prevent curling.

Dry, then peel off while warm and place on plastic wrap. Roll up, paper and all Store in tight container to keep pliable.

A dehydrator is best method. If a dehydrator is not available and sun is not hot enough, the oven may be used. Turn to 200°F. Leave door open a few inches. Place sheet in center of oven and turn front to back occasionally. Takes 4 to 6 hours. It is done when set. Cut in strips. Eat as a confection.

FRUIT SALAD LEATHER

Blend three or four ripe bananas, 1 cup applesauce, 1 cup crushed pineapple, 2 tbsp. Tang or any dehydrated orange ingredient, or 1 tbsp. lemon juice.

Variation: Combine finely chopped nuts with fruit mixture.

Pour out on very lightly oiled cookie sheet or on plastic wrap and dry.

FRUIT LEATHER ROLL UP

Filling:

1 cup dates, ground
1-2 tbsp. lemon juice
2 cups raisins, coarsely ground

3 tbsp. honey
2 cups walnuts, coarsely ground
2 tbsp. peanut butter

Mix all ingredients together. Spread out on fruit leather measuring 8 inches by 12 inches. Roll up like jelly roll. Chill and slice when ready to use. This amount of filling will make three rolls. Any leather can be used apple, peach, apricot, banana, or fruit salad. (See recipe for fruit salad leather.)

COCONUT COVERED RAISINS

½ cup honey
4 cups raisins, bleached white raisins
if available

1 cup toasted fine coconut

Warm honey and stir raisins into it. Then lift raisins out with slotted spoon, drop into coconut. Mix until well coated. Spread out on wax paper. Separate and cool.

HONEY, CAROB, NUT AND RAISIN SQUARES

1 cup honey
1½ cup powdered carob
1 cup powdered milk - noninstant

1 tsp. vanilla
2 cups raisins and cashews (any nut may be substituted)

Cook honey to soft ball stage. Blend a little of hot syrup into carob powder and return to heat. Cook a minute and remove from heat. Beat until warm. Mix in small amounts of powdered milk at a time. Add vanilla, nuts, and raisins. Mix well and press in pan. Cut in squares while still warm. Wrap each piece.

DRIED PEAR AND PINEAPPLE

Peal pears, scoop out seeds. Dip in heavy syrup, fill cavity with drained crushed pineapple. Dry. Serve sunny side, or cut side, up. A delicious confection.

Syrup for Drying Pears, heavy:

2 cups honey
1½ cups water

2 tsp. ascorbic acid powder

Heat and stir. Cool before dipping fruit.

FILLING FOR DATES

1 cup peanut butter
⅓ cup honey

3 tbsp. carob powder

Mix ingredients together. If too soft, add small amount of regular dry milk. Use also as filling for wrapping around a nut morsel or banana slices. Mix with chopped dried fruit and spread on graham crackers or plain cookies.

STUFFED DATES

Replace pit of date with pecan or walnut. Roll dates in mixture of ¼ cup warmed honey and 1 tbsp. lemon juice. Roll in fine coconut.

CAROB-COATED DATES

Stuff dates with nut half, either walnut or pecan. Pinch together and dip in carob coating that has been melted in a double boiler.

COCONUT-STUFFED DATES

Remove pits carefully from dates. Fill with walnut or pecan meat or coconut and honey mixture made by combining as much coconut as ½ cup solidified honey will take.

CAROB DATE NUT ROLL

Pit 24 dates and put them through a food grinder. Thoroughly mix the dates, 4 tbsp. carob powder, ½ tsp. sea salt, and enough honey to make the mixture sticky. Add 1 cup pecans or any raw nuts (ground) and form into a thin roll. Cover thickly with additional nuts if desired. Wrap in waxed paper and store in refrigerator. This may be sliced as needed.

PUFFED MILLET DATE BARS

1 cup raw sugar
1 egg beaten

1 cup chopped dates
¼ cup butter

Cook in double boiler until dates become soft - about 10 minutes - stirring constantly. Pour over 2 cups puffed millet. Press into square pan. Cut in squares, and press a pecan on top of each.

DATE CHOPSTICKS

3 cups dates
1 cup walnuts

½ cup shredded coconut
2 cups dried bananas

Run all ingredients through food grinder, using small blade. Roll into sticks 4 inches long. Wrap in wax paper.

COCONUT-ROLLED FIGS

1 cup toasted or plain coconut
½ cup honey

1 tbsp. lemon juice
1 lb. or more dark figs

Warm honey and lemon juice together. Stir in figs until well coated, then place figs in coconut and coat well.

STUFFED PRUNES

Pit prunes and fill with equal amounts of almond butter and hard honey or cream cheese and a walnut half, or basic candy mixture. Press a walnut, pecan, or almond into mixture.

Variation: Any nut butter can be used.

DRIED APRICOT AND APPLE BALLS

1 cup ground dried apricots
1 cup ground dried apples

2 tbsp. honey
¼ cup powdered milk

Mix honey and powdered milk together. Add fruit and form into small balls. Roll in fine coconut or crushed nuts. If fruit is too dry, pour warm water over and drain. Seal and let stand several hours. If necessary, repeat. This will make fruit easy to grind.

STUFFED DRIED APRICOTS

½ cup honey
1 ½ cups or less dry milk

1 cup grated coconut

Mix all ingredients together. Form into balls, flatten, and place between two apricot halves. This amount of filling will be sufficient for 2 lbs. of dried apricots.

CINNAMON APPLES (GLAZED)

1 cup honey

½ cup cinnamon candies or 2 to 3 drops oil of cinnamon and red food coloring

Melt honey and candies over medium heat, stirring and pressing candies with a spoon to dissolve them. Cook to hard ball stage, 255°F to 265°F. Remove from heat and dip dried apple rings or apple pieces into syrup individually. Cool on buttered cookie sheets.

DRIED PIE CHERRIES

Pit pie cherries. Dry until leathery. Stir around in warm honey. Lift out with slotted spoon. Drain slightly and roll in fine coconut or sugar.

DRIED FRUIT ROLL (SWEET)

1 cup figs
2 cups raisins
2 cups dates

2 cups dried apricots
1 cup walnuts coconut, fine

Grind fruit with meat grinder, using medium disk. Chop nuts and combine with fruit. Form into rolls and roll in fine coconut. Slice when ready to use.

DRIED FRUIT BALLS (TART)

1 cup raisins
1 cup prunes
1 cup figs

1 cup dates (dried peaches are good too)
2 tsp. lemon juice
1 cup chopped walnuts

Grind fruit. Add chopped nuts and lemon juice. Form into balls and roll in coconut.

Variation: Mix coconut in with fruits. ½ cup protein powder can be added for extra nourishment. Form balls and dip in carob coating. Delicious.

DRIED BANANA-NUT ROLL

1 cup dried bananas, ground
½ cup each: sesame, pumpkin, sunflower seeds (ground or blended)

1 cup nuts (pecans, walnuts, almonds, or cashews)

Chop nuts. Mix all ingredients together. Add 2 tbsp. lemon juice. Form roll. Chill and slice. If too moist, place on cookie sheet and dry out in 300°F oven for 5 minutes.

PECAN-STUFFED FIGS (CANDY FILLING)

¼ cup honey
1 tsp. lemon juice
½ tsp. vanilla

½ cup or more powdered milk, non-instant

Mix all ingredients together. Form small balls. Cut figs halfway through. Place ball of candy in and press half pecan into it.

Variation: Roll figs in fine coconut after stuffing or add coconut to candy filling, then stuff.

DRIED FRUIT AND HONEY SQUARES

1 cup raisins
1 cup dried prunes
1 cup figs

1 cup dates
1 cup nuts
1 cup hard granulated honey

Grind all fruit. Chop nuts. Blend both with hard honey. Press into square pan. Cut in squares and coat with coconut or powdered sugar.

SESAME SQUARES

Boil to hard crack stage, 300°F:
1 cup honey
1 tsp. vinegar

Cool slightly before adding seeds.
1 cup sesame seed
1 tsp. vanilla

Spread out in 8-inch-by-8-inch pan. Cut in squares. Cool.

YUM YUM SEED SQUARES

Grind or blend to a meal:

2 cups sesame seeds

1 cup sunflower seeds

Combine:

¼ cup carob powder

½ cup honey

½ cup hot water

¼ tsp. salt

½ tsp. vanilla

Add seed meal to carob mixture and spread out on cookie sheet. Dry in dehydrator or in 200°F oven with door ajar for 1 hour. Cut in squares. They will be chewy.

Variation: Add 1 cup coconut.

ORANGE OR GRAPEFRUIT STICKS

1 ½ cups raw or white sugar

¾ cups water

1 large grapefruit or 2 large oranges
(grapefruit more tender)

¼ tsp. salt

1-3 oz. package gelatin, raspberry or strawberry flavor

Peel fruit. Cut away some of white membrane, then cut peel into ¼-inch-by-2-inch strips. Measure 2 cups of strips. Cover with water and boil 20 minutes. Drain, add more water and repeat 2 more times. Drain. Combine sugar, water, and salt. Cook until sugar is dissolved. Add strips of peel and boil 20 minutes. Add gelatin and stir until dissolved. Lift peel out of syrup and let drain. After 20 minutes roll in fine coconut.

Dry for several hours. Store in can or jar.

RICE CRISPIE BALLS (UNCOOKED)

½ cup honey

½ cup powdered milk

½ cup peanut butter

½ tsp. vanilla

4 cups Rice Crispies

Heat honey. Remove from heat, add powdered milk, peanut butter, and vanilla. Mix thoroughly and pour over 4 cups Rice Crispies. Form into small balls. If desired, ⅓ cup carob chips can be added just before balls are formed.

SPROUTED WHEAT CAKES

2 cups sprouted wheat 48 hours old   ½ tsp. salt
1 cup nuts   3 tbsp. honey

Grind together and form into cookie. Dry in sun or in oven set at 200 F - door ajar.

WHEAT SPROUT BALLS

2 cups coarsely ground wheat sprouts   ½ tsp. salt
(48 hour)   1 cup ground almonds
1 cup ground raisins   (or other chopped nuts)
3 tbsp. honey

Form into balls, roll in fine coconut. Refrigerate if not eaten immediately.

Variation: Flatten balls that have been rolled in coconut. Bake on cookie sheet for 15-20 minutes at 350°F. The balls are also good rolled in toasted coconut.

48-hour sprouted wheat process: Spread soaked wheat on damp turkish towel. Cover with damp towel. Cover with plastic or paper. Sprinkle water often to keep towels damp but not soaking wet, or drain water off soaked wheat completely and leave in colander covered with wet cloth. Wash and drain once or twice a day. Sprout should not be longer than the grain.

BASIC RECIPE FOR BALLS

1 cup water   ½ cup honey
2 cups raw sugar

Cook to 260°F or very firm ball stage. Wash sides down with pastry brush dipped in hot water at first. Remove from heat. Add 1 tbsp. butter, ½ tsp. salt, 1 tsp. vanilla and pour over 4 cups of puffed rice and 1 cup Spanish peanuts. Form into balls and cool.

Variations for balls:
      1. Puffed wheat and toasted almonds.
      2. Toasted millet and coconut.
      3. Popcorn.
      4. Puffed rice and grated coconut.
      5. Puffed wheat and sliced dates.
      6. Cashews and puffed rice.

For sugared nuts, leave out honey and use cooked mixture on nuts or seeds such as pumpkin, sunflower, etc.

CARAMEL CORN

1½ cups brown sugar
1 square margarine
½ cup light karo

½ cup water
¼ tsp. cream of tartar

Cook to soft ball stage, 240°F. Add ¼ tsp. soda. Pour over 6 quarts popped corn. Spread on greased cookie sheet.

CAROB PUFFED RICE OR WHEAT

½ lb. carob coating
3 cups puffed rice or wheat

½ cup chopped toasted almonds

Melt carob over hot, not boiling, water. Mix with remaining ingredients and spread out to dry. Form in clusters if desired.

CAROB ALMOND BRITTLE

1¼ cups whole almonds
1 cup brown sugar
3 tbsp. roasted carob powder
½ cup honey

2 tbsp. water
¼ cup butter or margarine
½ tsp. soda
1 tsp. vanilla

Coarsely chop almonds and spread on a jelly roll pan and toast in 350°F oven about 8 minutes until lightly browned. Set aside. In a heavy saucepan mix sugar and carob powder. Add honey, water, butter and bring to boil stirring constantly. Continue cooking, stirring often, until syrup reaches 280°F, or hard crack stage on candy thermometer. Remove from heat and quickly stir in the nuts, soda, and vanilla. While still foaming, pour mixture onto buttered pan and spread until it is about ⅓-inch thick. Let stand until cool Break into pieces and store in airtight container. Makes about 1¼ pounds candy.

CAROB FRUIT AND NUT CANDY

1 lb. carob coating
3 cups sliced dates
3 cups raisins

1-2 cups toasted almonds, chopped coarsely

Melt carob over hot, not boiling, water. Add fruit and nuts. Drop in clusters on wax paper and cool. Toast almonds by mixing 1 tbsp. oil with nuts. Rub nuts between hands until coated. Bake on cookie sheet at 350°F for 20 minutes or until light tan on inside.

CAROB-COATED NUTS

Melt carob candy (plain carob squares, like chocolate) over hot water. Stir in any whole nuts, almonds, walnuts, cashews, etc. Separate and spread out on sheet and cool quickly.

SUGARED NUTS

1½ cups raw sugar
½ cup water
1 tbsp. butter
½ tsp. vanilla

1½ tsp. cinnamon
½ tsp. salt
1 lb. nuts, all one kind or mixed

Boil all ingredients to 236°F or soft ball stage. Remove from heat and stir in nuts. Stir until creamy, then spread on wax paper to cool. Break apart.

POPPED WHEAT

Preheat heavy skillet. Cover bottom with dry wheat, no oil. Shake until popping stops. Use plain in recipes calling for popped wheat. Add butter or oil and season wheat with salt, garlic salt, or onion salt and use as a wheat nut.

SPICED SUGARED COCONUT (FRESH)

1½ cups raw brown sugar
½ cup water
1 tbsp. butter

½ tsp. vanilla
1 to 1½ tsp. cinnamon
½ tsp. salt

Peel coconut and cut in thin strips. Boil above ingredients five minutes. Cool and pour over coconut. Stir until cool, then spread out on cookie sheet and place in oven. Bake for about 30 minutes at 325°F. Turn over once. Coconut will turn amber color. Remove from oven. Cool and separate. Store in can.

POPPED WHEAT DELUXE

Combine:
4 cups popped wheat
1 cup pumpkin seeds

1 cup sunflower seeds

Season with oil and salt.

WHEAT CRUNCH

½ cup honey
⅓ cup regular powdered milk
2 tbsp. water

½ tsp. vanilla
1 cup popped wheat
1 tbsp. peanut butter

Mix powdered milk and water to a paste. Cook honey to hard crack stage. Add milk mixture and stir well over heat for about 1 minute. Add vanilla, peanut butter, and popped wheat: Press in pan. Cool, cut in squares.

Variation: Add pecans for a special treat.

PARCHED WHEAT

Cook whole wheat as for cereal or pour boiling water over soaked wheat and put in thermos overnight. Drain off any remaining water. Spread out on cookie sheet and place under broiler for 10 minutes or until starts to pop. Set oven on bake and continue at 350°F for another 20 minutes or until crisp. Mix small. amounts of salad oil in warm wheat and season with salt, onion salt, or garlic salt. Canned cooked wheat can be used.

SOY NUTS (BAKED)

Soak soybeans 2 days in refrigerator. Cook with *live steam for two hours. Hulls will sluff off. Skim off, lift beans out. Place on cookie sheet. Place at least 8 inches under broiler in oven for about 20 minutes, stirring often. Turn oven to bake and continue to dry out at 300°F. Nuts are done when they are like peanuts. Work a little butter or oil into them and add salt.

*To cook soybeans in live steam, place a small pan inside a larger one. Add enough water in the large pan to come up halfway on the smaller one. Cover beans with water. Add 1 tsp. salt. Cover larger pan. Cook 2 hours. The live steam circulates around beans and cooks them faster than any other method.

SALTED SOYBEANS (DEEP FRIED)

Wash and soak dry beans overnight, drain and spread out to dry off. Place small amount of cooking oil in frying pan and heat to 450°F. Cover bottom of pan with beans and stir around for about 3 minutes or until golden brown color. Drain on paper towel. Salt while warm. Grind salted soybeans using medium fine blade. Use as topping for dessert, puddings, ice cream, or salads. Use to roll candies or dried fruit balls in.

SEED ROLL

1 cup sesame seeds
1 cup sunflower seeds
1 cup pumpkin seeds
1 cup peanuts
1 cup basic candy (see page 20)

1 cup almonds
1 cup pecans
2 cups raisins, finely ground
1 tbsp. lemon juice

Grind seeds rather fine. Chop or coarsely grind nuts and raisins. Add lemon juice to basic candy mixture, then add to seeds, nuts and raisins. Form in roll and chill. Slice.

SEED TREAT (UNCOOKED)

Grind to meal:
2 cups sesame seed
1 cup sunflower seed

Combine with:
¼ cup carob powder
½ cup honey
½ cup hot water

Spread out on cookie sheet and dry in oven or dehydrator. Cut in squares.

PROTEIN CONFECTION

1 cup raw wheat germ
1 cup sunflower seed meal* and ½ cup whole seeds
1 cup chopped raw nuts
1 cup sesame seed meal
1 cup powdered milk
3 cups quick cooking oatmeal (uncooked)

1 cup powdered date sugar or ground dates
1 cup honey
1 cup carob flour
½ cup soy flour
½ cup liquid milk
½ cup softened corn oil margarine

Warm honey, milk, ground dates, and margarine together for easier mixing. Mix all ingredients thoroughly before adding liquids. Form into walnut size balls. Roll in either powdered coconut, ground nuts, or sesame seeds to alleviate stickiness. Store in the refrigerator.

Three (3) balls equal approximately 25 calories. Six (6) balls have the protein value of a small steak.

*Obtain seed meals by either grinding finely or blending in a liquefier.

HALVAH (UNCOOKED)

½ cup unsweetened coconut
½ cup sunflower seed meal
½ cup wheat germ
¼ cup sesame seed

¼ cup honey
¼ cup powdered mik
¼ cup peanut butter

Mix all the ingredients together. Separate into two portions. Place each on a piece of waxed paper and form into a 1-inch roll. Wrap in waxed paper and keep in the refrigerator. Cut into 1-inch pieces as needed.

PEANUT MUNCH

Syrup:
1 cup brown sugar
½ cup molasses
½ cup water
pinch of salt (leave out salt if salted nuts are used)

1 cup raw peanuts
1 cup coconut, unsweetened
¼ cup oatmeal
¼ cup sunflower seeds

Boil syrup to soft ball stage, 250°F. Mix in remaining ingredients. Spread out buttered cookie sheets. Bake 30 minutes at 250°F. Remove from pan while still warm and let cool on wax paper. (Resembles Cracker Jack)

CANDIES

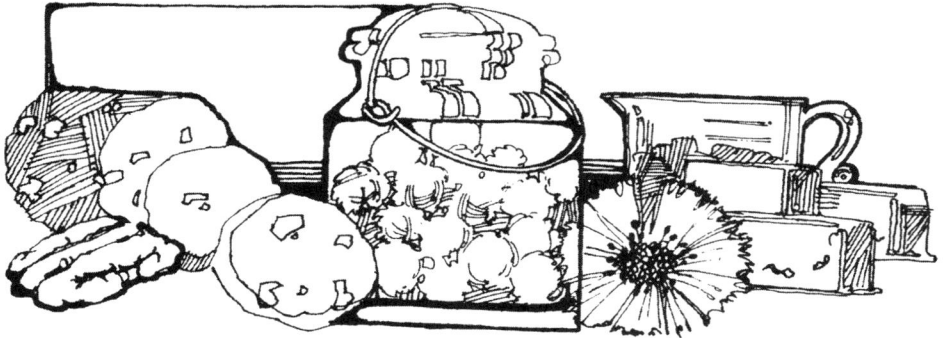

SIMPLE CANDIES

A good candy thermometer takes away the guesswork in candy making. A long-handled, flat wooden spoon is best for stirring and beating candy.

Wipe the sides of all candy pans down with pastry brush dipped in water while cooking. This helps to keep candy from crystallizing (going to sugar).

If crystallization takes place, most candies can be cooked over. If water is used, add more water. If cream or milk is used, add milk. Cook over low heat until dissolved, then continue as recipe directs. Divinity or nougat may be cooked more by beating over boiling water. Better success is attained by cooking candies fast. Where cream or milk is used, candy should be stirred constantly to keep from sticking. *These techniques are all-important.*

Stand thermometer up in pan while reading, not leaning against the side. This will make a big difference in degrees.

Testing without a thermometer:

Soft ball - small amount of candy dropped in cold water can be picked up.

Firm ball - small amount of candy dropped in cold water can be picked up. It will hold shape but can still be molded.

Hard ball - small amount of candy dropped in cold water. It will be difficult to mold.

Hard crack - small amount candy dropped in cold water. It will crackle when dropped in water or crack when hit against side of cup.

PREPARATION OF CAROB FOR DIPPING

Cut up carob and put in bowl over hot (not boiling) water to melt. Be sure the bowl is heat proof so it will not break. Be careful that no water or steam gets into carob. Stir often. When melted, pour some on marble slab, porcelain table top, Pyrex dish, or pie plates. Mix with hand until cool. Test carob by dipping fondant. If carob runs and makes a skirt around the base of dipped fondant, or dries too slowly, it is too warm. Continue mixing with hand until it is cool enough so that when fondant is dipped carob dries quickly. Gather carob in palm of hand, drop in ball of candy to be coated, roll toward fingers and shake off excess carob through fingers. Drop from fingertips onto waxed paper. Allow dipped fondant to stand for about one hour before boxing. When thin coating of carob is desired, dip candy in carob bowl while carob is slightly warm.

BASIC CANDY (UNCOOKED)

1½ cups noninstant dry milk   ½ cup honey, room temperature
1 tbsp. butter

Stir and knead enough *milk into honey to make a firm ball. Stretch and form into pencil size rolls. Let stand 3 to 4 hours. If rolls flatten out, gather up and knead more milk into it. Form into rolls and let stand again. Cut into bite-size pieces. If candy is to be stored, let pieces stand to dry slightly (to prevent sticking) before piling on top of each other.

Variations: Add peanut butter, nuts, coconut, dried fruit, carob, flavorings, food coloring, chocolate or carob chips, Rice Crispies. Add flavorings and food coloring to honey and mix well before adding milk. Try these combinations: Add 3 drops oil of peppermint (purchased at pharmacy) and ¼ tsp. green food coloring, ½ tsp. raspberry flavoring and ¼ tsp. red food coloring, ½ tsp. strawberry flavoring and ¼ tsp. red food coloring, ½ tsp. orange flavoring and ¼ tsp. combined red and yellow food coloring, or ½ tsp. black walnut flavoring.
*The amount of milk needed depends on the water content of the honey, which varies.

SWIRLS

1 recipe Basic Candy   ½ cup ground nuts

Spread mixture out thin. Spread finely ground nuts over mixture and press in slightly. Roll as for jelly roll Cut with string, making slices about ½ inch thick. Leave out in air to dry slightly before boxing.

Variation: Use ground, popped wheat in place of nuts. (See page 15)

CAROB DATE FUDGE (UNCOOKED)

2 scant cups powdered milk (noninstant)
1 cup honey
½ cup carob powder
2 tbsp. butter

1 tsp. vanilla
1 cup cut-up dates
1 cup nuts
coconut, fine

Blend together honey, butter, carob powder, and vanilla. Add dates and nuts. Form into balls and roll in fine coconut or press in pan and cut in squares.

Variation: Carob fudge. Omit dates and coconut, form into roll and let stand long enough to dry out before cutting into pieces.

CAROB CONFECTION (UNCOOKED)

¼ cup carob powder
½ cup honey
½ cup peanut butter
½ cup sunflower seeds

¼ cup wheat germ
¾ cup or more powdered milk
vanilla
coconut, fine

Mix honey, carob, milk, peanut butter, and vanilla well Add sunflower seeds and wheat germ. Form into balls and roll in coconut.

CAROB PEANUT BUTTER FUDGE (UNCOOKED)

1 cup peanut butter
1 cup honey
1 cup dry milk, noninstant

1 tsp. vanilla
1 cup carob powder (less if desired)
1 cup chopped nuts

Form into balls and roll in toasted coconut.

CAROB THINS (UNCOOKED)

½ cup honey
1½ cup powdered milk

1 tsp. vanilla
¼ lb. or less carob coating

Mix honey, milk, and vanilla together thoroughly. Press out flat or roll with rolling pin. Cut in half. Spread melted coating on half of candy. Cool and place remaining half on top. Cut in squares. To flavor carob with oil of peppermint, use 1 drop for ¼ lb. coating.

MOLASSES TAFFY (UNCOOKED)

2 tbsp. butter

1 cup molasses (Grandma's unsulfured)

2 cups noninstant powdered milk

Mix powdered milk with molasses and butter until it forms a stiff ball. Stretch and, if still sticky, mix in more dry milk and continue until very stiff. Stretch into a rope shape and cut in pieces and wrap.

Suckers are made by forming in the shape of a sucker, then dipping in carob coating.

BARBER POLES (UNCOOKED)

½ cup honey

1½ cup or more powdered milk, noninstant

Make 3 recipes of basic candy in three colors: red with raspberry flavoring; green with 3 drops oil of peppermint; orange, red and yellow coloring with orange flavoring. Add flavorings and food coloring to honey and mix thoroughly before adding milk. Mix and knead until smooth. Form into long thin rolls. Let stand to dry slightly. Twist three colors together. Cut, but let stand 3 or 4 hours to dry enough not to stick together when stored.

PEANUT BUTTER FUDGE (UNCOOKED)

Basic Recipe:

1 cup peanut butter

1 cup honey

1 cup dry milk, noninstant

1 tsp. vanilla

Mix all ingredients together. Press in pan, cut in squares. An almond on each square is good.

Variations: Roll small balls of mixture in toasted coconut. Chopped dried fruit may be added. Carob powder or carob chips added are good. 2 cups Rice Crispies mixed in, rolled into balls - delicious! Mix toasted coconut with basic recipe or roll balls of fudge in popped wheat.

SIMPLE PECAN ROLL (UNCOOKED)

1½ cups or more noninstant dry milk

1 tbsp. butter

1 tsp. vanilla

½ cup honey

Mix together thoroughly. Add 1 cup or more pecan pieces. Form in roll. Let stand overnight and slice.

BUTTERSCOTCH COCONUT BALLS (UNCOOKED)

1 cup coconut
1 cup powdered milk, noninstant
½ tsp. vanilla

½ cup honey
2 tbsp. margarine or butter

Brown coconut and dry milk in 250°F oven, using separate pie tins, and stirring often. When they are light gold in color, remove and cool before adding to honey and margarine. Form into balls.

Variation: Add ½ cup walnuts or pecans.

CAROB COCONUT FUDGE (UNCOOKED)

1 cup peanut butter
1 cup honey
1 cup carob powder

1 tsp. vanilla
2 cups grated coconut

Mix all ingredients together and cut in squares or roll in balls.

ALL-DAY SUCKERS (COOKED)

1 cup honey

1½ cups powdered milk

Cook honey to hard crack stage. Pour, stirring at same time, gradually into powdered milk. Roll into small balls. Insert sucker sticks. For root beer flavor, add 4 tbsp. root beer extract to cooked honey before adding honey to powdered milk. Add more powdered milk as necessary.

ENERGY CHEWS

1 cup mild molasses (Grandma's)
1 cup raw or brown sugar
1 cup sunflower seeds

1 cup sesame seeds
1 tbsp. butter
1 tsp. vanilla

Cook molasses and sugar to 250°F. Add remaining ingredients and stir well. Spread out in cake pan. Cut when cool and wrap. (Caramel-like).

WHITE LICORICE CHEWS

1 cup honey
1 tbsp. butter

12 drops of oil of anise

Cook honey to hard ball stage, 250°F. Add 1 tbsp. butter and oil of anise. Pour out on buttered platter. Cool and stretch. Cut and wrap.

HONEY TAFFY

1½ cups honey
1 tbsp. cream

1 tbsp. butter
1 tsp. vanilla

Place honey and butter in pan and cook until it spins thread - firm ball, 245°F. Remove from heat, add cream and vanilla. Mix and pour on buttered slab. Cool and pull. If undercooked, add powdered milk and continue to pull until it holds its shape when stretched out.

MOLASSES DREAMS (UNCOOKED)

1 cup mild molasses
1 cup peanut butter

1 cup or more powdered milk, noninstant

Mix thoroughly. Form in balls and top with a pecan.

MOLASSES TAFFY

1 cup brown or raw sugar
1 cup molasses, mild

½ cup water

Mix all ingredients and boil to hard ball stage, 245°F. Remove and add 2 tbsp. butter, ¼ tsp. soda, few grains salt. Pour out on buttered platter, cool and stretch.

Variation: Equal amounts of honey and molasses can be used. Eliminate raw sugar.

CARAMEL JOYS

1 recipe Caramel (see page 25)
1 cup toasted almond pieces

1 recipe Brown Sugar Fondant
(see page 30)

Spread cooled fondant in 12-inch square buttered pan. Sprinkle almonds on top. Pour hot caramel over, cool, cut in squares. Dip if desired in carob also good without.

SPUN PEANUT BRITTLE

2 cups raw sugar
¼ cup honey
1 cup water

2 cups raw peanuts
(dash of salt if raw peanuts are used)

Boil sugar, honey, water, and salt to 300°F, or hard crack stage. Wash sides of pan down with pastry brush dipped in hot water as mixture comes to boil. Add 2 cups peanuts or less. Remove from heat, add ¼ lb. butter, 1½ tsp. soda, 2 tsp. vanilla. Pour out on cookie sheets as soon as it begins to set, pull out with fork and fingers until it is very thin. Break when cool.

RAW SUGAR TAFFY

1 cup raw sugar
¼ cup honey
½ cup water

1 cup powdered milk
1 tsp. vanilla

Cook sugar, water and honey to 236°F or soft ball stage. Remove and stir until almost cool. Add vanilla and 1 cup powdered milk or enough more to make it possible to stretch. Stretch for a few minutes and layout in rope shape. When cool, cut in pieces.

MOLASSES CASHEW TAFFY

1 cup molasses
2 tbsp. cashew butter

¼ to ½ cup powdered milk, noninstant

Cook molasses until it reaches firm ball stage, 242°F. Pour onto buttered platter. Cool. Work in powdered milk until of stretchable consistency. Add cashew butter and stretch until blended in. Form in rope shape and cut.

HONEY CARAMELS

2 cups honey
1 cup evaporated milk
1 tsp. vanilla

3 tbsp. butter
pinch of salt
1 cup chopped nuts or more.

Mix honey and evaporated milk together. Cook, stirring constantly, to a firm ball stage, 255°F. Stir in butter and nuts and salt. Pour onto a buttered square cake pan. Cool and cut into pieces.

Caramel Apples: Dip apples (dry and crisp) into cooked caramel and spoon excess off bottom before drying on greased cookie sheets.

CAROB BLACK CROW SUCKERS

1 cup honey
½ cup carob powder or ⅓ lb. carob bar

1 cup powdered milk
1 tsp. vanilla

Cook honey to hard ball stage, 255°F. Remove from heat and mix in carob, vanilla, and powdered milk. Stir until smooth and cool enough to handle. Form suckers over sticks. Cool and wrap.

WHEAT PORCUPINES

1 cup peanut butter
1 cup honey

1 cup or more powdered milk
(noninstant)

Blend together. Form in balls and roll in popped wheat (see page 15).

CAROB "TOOTSIE ROLLS"

1 cup honey
½ cup carob powder or ⅓ lb. carob bar

1 cup powdered milk noninstant
1 tsp. vanilla

Cook honey to hard ball stage, 255°F. Remove from heat. Stir in carob and vanilla thoroughly, then add powdered milk. Blend well. Cool enough to handle and form into a roll the size of a pencil. Cut into 2-inch pieces and wrap.

HONEY CANDY

2 cups honey
1 cup brown sugar

1 cup cream

Combine honey, sugar, and cream and cook slowly until it reaches the hard ball stage, 255°F, when tested in cold water. Pour onto buttered platter and cool. When cool enough to handle, butter hands and pull until a golden color. Cut into pieces and wrap individually in wax paper.

MOLDED CAROB CANDIES

½ lb. carob bar

1 cup fine unsweetened coconut

Melt carob over hot, but not boiling water. Stir in coconut and press in small molds. Small animal molds can be purchased at import stores. If not available, use bottoms of small individual jello molds or cups. (Cool and unmold.)

HONEY WHEAT CRISPIES

1 cup honey
1 tbsp. butter
1 tsp. vanilla

1 tsp. soda
2 cups popped wheat (see page 15)

Cook honey to hard crack stage, 300°F. Remove from heat. Add butter, vanilla, and soda. Pour in 2 cups popped wheat. Pour out in buttered cookie sheet. Cut before cool, or break into pieces.

Variations: Before pouring into cookie sheet, add 2 tbsp. peanut butter, or any other nut butter desired.

SESAME HONEY CANDY

1 cup honey
1 tsp. vinegar

½ tsp. vanilla
2 cups sesame seeds

Boil honey and vinegar to hard crack stage, 300°F. Do not burn. Remove from heat, add vanilla. Cool slightly and add sesame seeds, plain or toasted. Cool in buttered pan, dripper size or cookie sheet. Cut in small squares while still warm.

POPPED WHEAT FLOUR CANDY

½ cup popped wheat flour
(pop wheat and grind into fine flour)
1 cup honey

½ tsp. vanilla
2 tbsps. peanut butter

Mix all together. Form into a roll or press into square pan and cut.

Variations: Add toasted coconut, nuts, dates or raisins, wheat germ, etc.

Fancy Candies
(READ GENERAL TIPS FOR COOKED CANDIES)

CAROB DROPS

1 can chinese noodles
2 cups carob chips or carob coating

1 cup butterscotch chips
1 cup nuts

Melt carob and butterscotch chips over hot water. Add nuts and noodles. Drop from a spoon into clusters. Cool.

LIGHT FUDGE

2 cups raw or brown sugar
½ cup cream or canned milk
⅓ cup milk, fresh
1 tbsp. honey

¼ square butter
1 tsp. vanilla
about 1 cup powdered milk
1 cup nuts, walnuts or pecans

Cook first four ingredients to 220°F. Wash sides of pan down with pastry brush dipped in hot water. Pour out on slab or platter. Cool. Beat until creamy, add butter and vanilla, then add dry noninstant powdered milk until it can be formed into a ball. Add nuts. Form in roll and wrap in foil. Cut when ready to eat.

MAPLE CREAMS

1 recipe light fudge with ½ tsp. maple flavoring added.

Cool and form into balls. Roll in toasted coconut or plain, fine untoasted coconut.

WALNUT CRUNCH (LIKE TOFFEE)

1 cup raw sugar
3 tbsp. water
1 tbsp. honey

⅓ cup margarine or butter
¾ cup finely chopped walnuts
1 square or 2 oz. carob, grated

Combine sugar, water, honey, and margarine. Cook over low heat until dissolved, then turn heat up and continue boiling without stirring to hard crack stage, 260°F. Pour over ½ cup nuts on greased pie tin. Sprinkle grated carob over top and spread around. Top with remaining nuts. Cool and break. Yields ¾ lb.

MOLASSES CARAMELS

1½ cups sugar, raw or brown
1 cup molasses
½ cup honey

1 cup cream or canned milk
piece of butter, size of walnut
1 cup or more of nut meats

Boil to hard ball stage, 255°F. stirring constantly. Remove from fire and stir in 1 cup nut meats. Pour in pan. Cool and cut in 1-inch squares.

PENOCHE COCONUT BALLS

2 cups raw or brown sugar
1 tbsp. honey
pinch salt

¾ cup cream or canned milk
2 tbsp. butter, to be added later
1 tsp. vanilla

Combine all ingredients except butter and vanilla and cook to 224°F. Wipe sides down with pastry brush dipped in hot water at beginning and end of cooking. Pour out on slab. Cool and beat until creamy. Add butter and vanilla Cool in refrigerator, then form into balls and roll in toasted coconut.

CAROB FUDGE

2 cups raw sugar
½ cup cream or canned milk
⅓ cup homogenized milk
1 tbsp. honey

¼ cup carob powder
¼ square butter
1 tsp. vanilla
nuts

Combine sugar, milk or cream, honey, and carob powder in pan. Bring to a boil over medium heat, stirring constantly. Wipe sides of pan down with pastry brush dipped in hot water. Repeat again later. Turn heat up and cook to 224°F or soft ball, stirring constantly. Pour out onto slab. Cool. Beat until it starts to lose its gloss. Add butter and knead with palm of hand. Add vanilla and mix in well. Add nuts. Form in roll and cut when ready to use.

PECAN ROLL

1 recipe Light Fudge (see page 28)

1 recipe Caramel (see page 25)
pecans

Spread pecans on buttered cookie sheet. Pour hot caramel over pecans. Cool. Cut into 8-inch-by-3-inch strips. Form small 8-inch rolls of light fudge. Place roll on caramel and bring edges together up over it.

PECAN ROLL (COOKED)

Cooked:
2 cups coarsely chopped pecans
1 recipe Honey Caramel (see page 25)

Uncooked:
1 cup or more powdered milk
½ cup honey
1 tsp. vanilla
1 tbsp. butter
pinch of salt

Sprinkle nuts on well-buttered cookie sheet. Pour hot caramel over nuts and cool. Mix together honey, powdered milk, vanilla, salt, and butter. Flatten out to approximately size of caramel and nut mixture, lift and place on top. Roll like jelly roll. If too thick, pull out longer. Slice.

BROWN SUGAR FONDANT

2 cups brown sugar
¾ cup light cream or canned milk
1 tbsp. honey

2 tbsp. butter
1 tsp. vanilla
1 cup walnuts (nuts optional)

Cook sugar, cream, and honey to 225°F. Wash sides down with pastry brush dipped in hot water at least twice during cooking. Pour out on slab. Cool and beat until creamy. Add butter, vanilla, and nuts. Knead with heel of hand. Form into rolls and slice when ready to use or form into balls and dip in carob coating.

ALMOND DREAMS

1 recipe of Light Fudge (see page 28)
¾ lbs. carob coating

½ lb. almonds, toasted and crushed or ground finely

Form cooked light fudge into small balls. Cool. Melt carob coating over hot water (not boiling), cool and dip balls in, then roll in nuts.

TURTLES

1 recipe caramel cooked to the soft ball stage (230°F)

pecans
carob coating

Place pecan halves in twos on buttered cookie sheets - spoon about 1 tbsp. hot caramel over each two nuts. Cool in refrigerator. While still very firm, dip in carob coating.

DIVINITY (RAW SUGAR)

4 cups raw sugar
1 cup water
¼ cup honey
pinch of salt

4 egg whites (or ½ cup), beaten stiff but not dry
1 tsp. vanilla
1 cup nuts

Cook first four ingredients to 245°F. Add syrup gradually to egg whites, beating until it loses its gloss. Add vanilla and nuts and spoon out.

Variations: Carob chips can be added after candy has cooled and is ready to spoon out.

APPLETS, COTLETS, OR GRAPELETS (GELATIN CANDY)

2 tbsp. plain gelatin dissolved in ½ cup applesauce
¾ cup cold applesauce

2 cups raw or brown sugar
1 cup walnuts
1 tsp. vanilla

Soak gelatin in ½ cup applesauce for 10 minutes. Combine remaining applesauce and sugar and boil 10 minutes. Add gelatin mixture and boil 15 minutes longer, stirring constantly. Take off heat, add vanilla and nuts and pour into buttered 8-inch-by-8-inch pan. Let stand overnight. Cut into squares and roll in powdered sugar or dip in carob coating. When making cotlets or grapelets, cook apricot or grape puree until fairly thick before measuring.

ALMOND CARAMEL JOYS

1 cup powdered milk
½ cup honey
1 cup shredded moist coconut

1 tsp. vanilla
¼ tsp. salt
1 recipe caramels (see page 25)

Mix honey, milk, salt, and vanilla together. Add coconut and press in small square pan. Add 1 cup chopped toasted almonds on top. Pour layer of hot caramel over all. Cool. Cut in squares and dip in carob coating.

HONEY MARSHMALLOWS (UNCOOKED)

¾ cup raw or brown sugar
1 cup honey
1½ tbsp. unflavored gelatin
⅓ cup water

¼ tsp. salt
1 tsp. vanilla
2 cups nuts, walnuts or pecans

Pour water in small saucepan and sprinkle gelatin on top. Let stand 5 minutes. Place pan over medium heat and stir only until dissolved. Add raw sugar and continue stirring until it is dissolved. Do not boil. Add honey, salt, and vanilla. Transfer all to a bowl and beat with electric beater until cool and tacky. Add nuts, fruit, etc. Any of the following are good: coconut, carob chips, chopped dried apricots, raisins, or currants. Sprinkle powdered milk or powdered sugar on bottom of square cake pan. Pour candy into pan and spread evenly. Let stand a few hours before cutting with a hot knife.

Roll squares in toasted coconut or popped wheat, or dip squares in carob coating. Roll dipped candy in toasted or plain coconut or, best yet, toasted, ground almonds. Have fun!

CARAMEL (TENDER)

½ lb. butter
2 cups brown sugar
2 cups honey

2 cans evaporated milk
1 tsp. vanilla

Melt butter, add honey then sugar. Bring to a boil. Add milk a little at a time so candy doesn't stop boiling. Cook to firm ball stage (235°F). Pour into buttered trays. This candy must be stirred constantly. Cook in heavy gauge pan on high heat until almost done, then lower to medium heat to prevent sticking. Makes a large batch.

CAROB MINT SANDWICHES

1 lb. fine-textured carob bar
4 oz. green coating

3 tbsp. vegetable shortening
oil of peppermint flavoring

Melt carob and green coating separately over hot water (not boiling). Mix 2 tbsp. of the shortening and 5 drops peppermint flavoring in carob. Place wax paper in cake pan. Pour half of the carob in pan and spread evenly. Set aside to set up - not hard. Meanwhile, mix 1 tbsp. shortening and 2 drops flavoring in green coating. When carob is set, spread green coating over carob and let set. Spread remaining carob over green. Let set firm and cut in 1-inch squares.

DESSERTS

FRUIT SALAD DRESSING

1 cup pineapple juice
2 tbsp. frozen orange juice
1 tsp. lemon juice
2 tbsp. honey

1 egg
1½ tbsp. cornstarch
pinch salt

Beat egg slightly. Combine with cornstarch, salt, and honey in top of double boiler. Add juices. Cook slowly until mixture thickens. Cool before using. Combine with 1 cup whipping cream or 1 pkg. whipped topping mix. Sweeten with additional honey if necessary. Use with fruit salad or as topping for fresh fruit plate.

FLUFFY HONEY DRESSING

2 eggs
½ cup honey
¼ cup lemon juice
2 tbsp. frozen orange juice concentrate

⅛ tsp. salt
½ cup whipping cream, whipped
2 tsp. grated lemon peel

In a small saucepan beat eggs. Stir in honey, lemon juice, orange juice concentrate, and salt. Cook over low heat, stirring constantly until thickened. Cool. Fold in whipped cream and lemon peel. Serve with strawberries, banana slices, apple wedges, pineapple chunks, etc., and garnish with a sprig of peppermint. Makes 2 cups dressing.

LEMON SAUCE

3 tbsp. cornstarch
2 egg yolks, beaten
1 cup honey
pinch of salt

1 tbsp. butter
2 cups boiling water
juice of 1½ lemons

Stir cornstarch, egg yolks, and honey together. Add boiling water, lemon juice, and butter, and cook until thick. Use on carrot or English pudding.

HONEY CREAM SAUCE

Mix in small saucepan:
2 tbsp. melted butter
2 tsp. cornstarch

½ cup honey

Cook 5 minutes (for puddings, ice cream toppings, etc.).

PINEAPPLE HONEY DRESSING

Mix and shake well:
½ cup honey
¼ cup lemon juice
¼ tsp. salt

3 tbsp. crushed pineapple
 (for fruit salads)

OLD-FASHIONED FRUIT SALAD

1 cup canned pie cherries, drained*
3 bananas, ripe but firm
1½ cups pineapple tidbits or pieces of
fresh pineapple

1 orange, peeled and cut in small pieces
½ cup shredded coconut
2 medium size apples, preferably
Jonathan, peeled and diced

Combine with Fruit Salad Dressing (see page 33).

*Use juice from cherries as part of liquid in the fruit salad dressing.

DRIED FRUIT PUDDING

Use any dried fruit available. Peaches and apricots are best. Soak dried fruit in water for 6 hours, until soft. Bring to boil, sweeten with honey, add tapioca, cinnamon, and 1 tbsp. butter. Three cups of liquid will require ¼ cup tapioca. Cook until clear. Cool. Top with whipped cream or whipped powdered milk.

WHIPPED POWDERED MILK

1 cup ice water   1 cup noninstant powdered milk

Whip until thick. Add 1 tsp. lemon juice. Sweeten to taste. Flavor with vanilla.

DANISH SWEET SOUP

3 cups dried prunes soaked   ½ cup minute tapioca
3 cups raisins   2 tsp. vanilla
1 cup dried apples   4 tbsp. butter
1 cup honey   2 sticks cinnamon
⅛ tsp. salt   or 2 tsp. ground cinnamon

Cover fruit with water and boil until soft. Add honey, tapioca, butter, vanilla and cinnamon. Add enough more water to make 1½ quarts of liquid. Serve hot or cold. Use any dried fruit combination. Apricots and peaches are a good color combination.

POOR MAN'S PUDDING

¼ cup shortening   ½ tsp. salt
1½ cups whole wheat flour   ½ cup milk
½ cup honey   ½ cup raisins
½ tsp. soda   ½ cup nuts (optional)
1 tsp. baking powder   ½ tsp. cinnamon

Blend shortening and honey, add milk then dry ingredients and raisins. Spread out in cake pan. Dissolve 1 cup brown sugar in 2 cups hot water. Pour over batter and bake at 350°F for 30 minutes.

Variation: Dates may be substituted for the raisins.

CARROT PUDDING

2 cups raisins   1 egg
1 cup whole wheat flour   1 tsp. soda
1 cup honey   ½ tsp. baking powder
1 cup soft bread crumbs   1 tsp. each allspice, cinnamon
1 cup nuts, chopped   ½ tsp. salt
1 cup grated carrots

Mix all ingredients together just enough to moisten. Fill greased cans three-fourths full. Put lids on and steam for three hours.

RICE PUDDING

2 cups cooked brown rice
3 cups milk
⅔ cup honey

3 eggs, slightly beaten
1 cup raisins
nutmeg

Mix rice, milk, and honey. Add the eggs. Stir in the raisins. Sprinkle nutmeg on top. Bake in greased baking dish for about one hour.

HEALTH PUDDING

1 cup whole wheat flour
1 cup graham cracker crumbs
1 tsp. soda
½ tsp. cinnamon
½ tsp. nutmeg
½ tsp. salt

½ cup honey
¼ cup butter
1 cup milk
½ cup raisins
½ cup nuts

Mix dry ingredients together. Heat honey, butter, and milk together and pour into dry ingredients and mix well. Steam 1 hour or more in buttered cans. Serve warm with sauce.

Health Pudding Sauce:

1 cup brown sugar
¼ cup butter
3 cups milk

1/4 tsp. salt
vanilla
2 tbsp. (scant) cornstarch

Mix cornstarch in small amount of the milk Bring remaining ingredients to boil, add cornstarch. Cooking in a double boiler will prevent sticking.

HONEY BREAD PUDDING

2 cups day-old bread cubes
¼ cup honey
2 tbsp. margarine
⅛ tsp. salt

2 eggs, beaten
½ tsp. vanilla
1⅔ cups hot milk
½ cup raisins (optional)

Place bread cubes in small baking dish. Combine the honey, margarine, salt, eggs, and vanilla. Slowly stir in the milk. Pour the mixture over the bread. Set baking dish in a pan of hot water and bake 350°F for 30 to 40 minutes or until pudding is set.

ENGLISH PLUM PUDDING

1 cup brown sugar
1½ cups whole wheat flour
1¾ cups bread crumbs
½ cup molasses, mild
1 cup ground suet
2 eggs
1 cup sour milk
1 cup raisins
1 cup nuts

1 cup currants
1 tsp. soda
1 tsp. cinnamon
½ tsp. cloves
½ tsp. nutmeg
½ tsp. salt
1 tsp. vanilla
¼ lb. fruit mix

Combine all fruit and nuts and dredge with flour. Add spices to flour, then nuts, brown sugar, bread crumbs, and beaten eggs in order. Add soda and milk to mixture. Add fruit mixture last. Fill oiled cans two-thirds full. Place lid on and steam 3 hours.

HONEY CUSTARD

¼ tsp. salt
3 eggs beaten
¼ cup honey

2 cups milk
nutmeg

Scald milk, add honey, salt, and slightly beaten eggs. Pour into custard cups. Top with sprinkle of nutmeg. Set cups in pan of hot water. Bake 325°F for 40 minutes or until custard is firm.

TAPIOCA CREAM

⅓ cup quick-cooking tapioca
½ cup honey
¼ tsp. salt

2 eggs
4 cups milk, scalded
1 tsp. vanilla

Combine tapioca, honey, salt, and egg yolks in top of double boiler. Add scalded milk, slowly. Cook and stir until tapioca is transparent. Remove from heat and fold in stiffly beaten egg whites. Add vanilla. Good served either warm or cold.

PRIZE FRUIT PLATE

Use fruits in season: watermelon, cantaloupe, grapes, bananas, peaches, pears, strawberries or any other fresh fruit available. Arrange on platter or pile assorted fruits in cantaloupe half shell. Top with fruit salad dressing. (See Fruit Salad Dressing page. 33)

FRUIT COBBLER

¼ cup margarine
1 cup honey
1 egg separated
½ cup milk
½ tsp. vanilla

1 cup whole wheat flour
¼ tsp. salt
2 tsp. baking powder
3 cups berries, cherries or other fruit
1 cup fruit juice

Mix half of the honey with butter, egg yolk, milk, and vanilla. Add dry ingredients and beat well Add beaten egg whites last. Drizzle remaining half cup honey over fruit. (If pie cherries or other tart fruits are used, add more honey.) Spread batter in cake pan first. Place fruit on top of batter. Pour 1 cup juice over all Bake 350°F for 30 minutes.

APPLE CAKE PUDDING

1 cup whole wheat flour
1 tsp. soda
1 tsp. cinnamon
¼ tsp. salt
¾ tsp. nutmeg

¼ cup margarine
1 cup raw sugar
1 egg, beaten
2 cups grated apples, packed firm

Cream shortening and sugar, add eggs and apples. Then add dry ingredients. Pour into 8-inch-by-8-inch pan. Top with ½ cup walnuts chopped, mixed with ½ cup brown sugar, 2 tbsp. melted butter. Sprinkle on batter, press gently. Bake at 325°F for about 45 minutes. Serve warm with your favorite sauce. Butterscotch pudding mix cooked and thinned down, is good, or use Caramel Sauce (see page 39-40).

APPLE DESSERT

½ cup honey
½ cup brown sugar
½ cup butter
1 egg
3 or 4 medium apples, diced fine
½ cup nuts

1½ cup whole wheat flour
1 tsp. soda
1 tsp. cinnamon
1 tsp. nutmeg
½ tsp. salt

Cream butter, add honey and egg and beat well. Add apples, stir, add sifted dry ingredients, then add nuts last. Bake in 8-inch-by-8-inch pan 325°F to 350°F about 40 minutes. Serve with Caramel Sauce (see page 39-40).

QUICK CAROB PUDDING

1 cup water
3 eggs
¼ cup honey
¼ cup cream (or canned milk)

¼ cup oil (soy or safflower)
3 tbsp. carob powder
1 tsp. vanilla
¼ tsp. salt

Bring water to a boil. Stir in beaten eggs and stir until thick as thin mush. Pour into blender, add other ingredients, blend 1 minute. May be frozen for fudgesicles, used as pie filling or as pudding. Great as a sauce for cake or ice cream, or served warm on ice cream topped with granola.

CARAMEL SAUCE

1 cup brown sugar
2 tbsp. cornstarch

2 tbsp. butter
juice of 1 lemon
1½ cups boiling water

Blend brown sugar and cornstarch together. Add water, butter and lemon juice. Cook until thick

RHUBARB CRUNCH

Crumb Topping:
1 cup sifted whole wheat flour
1 cup brown sugar, packed
⅔ cup melted butter or margarine
¾ cup uncooked rolled oats
1 tsp. cinnamon

Fruit Mixture:
4 cups diced rhubarb
2 tbsp. cornstarch
1 tsp. vanilla
1 cup honey
1 cup water

Mix crumb topping ingredients until crumbly. Press half of crumbs in 9-inch greased pan. Cover with rhubarb. Combine honey, cornstarch, water, and vanilla, and cook till thick and clear. Pour over rhubarb and top with remaining crumbs. Bake at 350°F for 1 hour. Serve warm with whipped cream or ice cream. Makes 8 servings.

PINEAPPLE BOAT

Cut ripe pineapple in half lengthwise. Cut down sides and lift fruit out in strips. Scrape out remaining pulp. Combine with any fruits in season and pile back into pineapple shell. Garnish with fresh mint. Chicken salad piled in pineapple with strips of pineapple alongside is a perfect luncheon dish.

PEACH CRISP

4 cups peaches, sliced
½ tsp. cinnamon
⅔ cup honey
1 cup whole wheat flour

¼ cup brown sugar
½ stick margarine
½ tsp. salt

Peel peaches, place in shallow baking dish. Drizzle honey over peaches and sprinkle cinnamon on top. Mix flour and brown sugar, salt, and margarine. Sprinkle on top of peaches. Bake 375°F for 30 minutes.

CARAMEL SAUCE (NO BROWN SUGAR)

1 cup dry milk
1 cup honey

½ cup water
½ tsp. vanilla

Mix together until smooth then cook in top of double boiler for 45 minutes, stirring often.

Variations: For German chocolate cake filling, add 1 cup pecans, ½ cup coconut, 1 tbsp. butter. Or add 1 cup ground dates and ½ cup walnuts, and use as topping on spice cake.

APPLE SURPRISE

6 apples, tart
¾ cup honey

1 cup water
1 tsp. cinnamon

Peel, slice, and cook apples with honey, water, and cinnamon for 10 minutes. Put in 8-inch-by-8-inch square pan. Top with 6 tbsp. margarine, ½ cup brown sugar, 1 cup whole wheat flour, 1 tsp. baking powder, ¼ tsp. salt. Blend sugar and margarine, add flour, baking powder, and salt, and work in. Sprinkle on top of apples. Bake 350°F for 45 minutes. Serve with whipped cream or ice cream.

PEACH BROWN BETTY

2 cups whole wheat bread crumbs
4 cups sliced peaches

½ cup brown sugar
1 tsp. lemon juice and ½ tsp. vanilla

Mix fruit, sugar, lemon juice and vanilla together. Place layer of crumbs in baking dish then layer of fruit, alternating layers. Bake 30 minutes at 350°F. Top with whipped cream.

Variation: Apples and raisins may be substituted for peaches.

DATE CEREAL ROLL (UNCOOKED)

3 cups bran flakes
1 cup corn flakes
¼ cup sugar, brown
1 tsp. grated orange rind

1 cup finely cut dates
1 cup broken walnuts
1 cup milk

Crush cereal flakes, set aside ½ cup. Combine remaining crumbs with other ingredients in order given. Place mixture on wax paper and shape into roll about 8-inch long. Sprinkle outside with the ½ cup corn flakes. Wrap in wax paper and chill 5 to 6 hours. Cut in slices and top with whipped cream.

WHEAT AND RAISINS

1 cup raisins
2 cups water
3 tbsp. honey (or more to taste)
1 tbsp. vinegar

2 tbsp. cornstarch
1 tbsp. butter
4 cups cooked whole wheat

Boil raisins until soft. Add vinegar, honey, butter. Thicken with cornstarch. Combine with wheat (steamed is softer). Good served hot or cold as pudding or cereal.

Variations: Substitute dried apricots, prunes, peaches, etc., for raisins. Adjust honey to taste.

DATE SUGAR USES

Date sugar is a wonderful natural sweet and can be used in various ways. Sprinkle it on top of whipped cream, meringue and puddings or include it in ether desserts, such as in the crumb part of Apple Surprise, in Health Pudding, and Poor Man's Pudding. Use it in cookies, bars and cakes. Add it to candies for interesting textures and flavor. It can be used as sweetener for Dried Fruit Balls, Leather Roll Ups or seed and nut rolls. Try it sprinkled on cereals or in granola.

It has not been included in the recipes because it is not always available. Inquire about it at your natural food stores or write to date companies for price lists. Increased demand will make it more available.

FRESH FRUIT DESSERT IDEAS

Fruit combinations, fresh or canned:

1. Watermelon squares (5" x 5" x 1") with cantaloupe balls piled on top and garnish with sprig of mint.
2. Cantaloupe ring served with grapes in center or use watermelon balls. Place ring on grape leaves.
3. Melon ball fruit cocktail: various melon balls in sherbet dish with orange juice over all.
4. Fresh fruit cocktail: pineapple cubes, orange segments, grapes, apples, and banana. Serve with lemon-orange freeze (lemon and orange juice and ice in blender).
5. Fresh fruit arrangement: strawberries, fresh pineapple, and bananas served on platter.
6. Fresh fruit arrangement served in tiered dish, grapes (hanging from top tier), cantaloupe and watermelon chunks, strawberries and bananas.
7. Whole apples, plums, peaches, pears, bananas, etc. Serve on platter with paring knife.
8. Crushed orange: cut top out, loosen orange pulp and fill with cracked ice or additional juice. You'll be surprised at this simple treat.
9. Grilled grapefruit: cut open grapefruit and section. Sprinkle brown sugar over and broil Garnish with half a cherry or any fresh berry.
10. Fresh raspberries: serve in small dessert dish all by themselves.
11. Stewed rhubarb: cook with honey, raspberry flavoring, and a few drops of red food coloring.
12. Strawberry milkshake: ¼ cup powdered milk, honey, 6 frozen strawberries or fresh strawberry flavoring, ½ cup water. Blend and add ice cubes till it is slushy. Any other berries can be used. Lemon juice heightens the flavor.
13. Orange freeze: orange juice, lemon juice, honey. Blend and add ice cubes. Blend to a freeze consistency.
14. Blueberry freeze: orange juice, blueberries, lemon juice, honey, ice cubes. Blend to a slush.
15. Gelatin blueberry: follow directions on Knox Gelatin box for 1 packet. Add blue berries, honey, lemon, and set. Canned, unsweetened pineapple also can be substituted for blueberries.
16. Raspberry or strawberry fluff: Whip canned, skim milk until stiff. Add berries and flavoring, sweetener, and a dash of salt. Make up 1 packet gelatin, cool to syrupy consistency. Whip and combine with above. Set. Can be used as pie filling.
17. Fresh pureed fruit set in plain unflavored gelatin. Heighten flavor with lemon juice or sweeten with honey as needed.

COOKIES AND BARS

CHEWY COCONUT SQUARES

First part:
½ cup brown sugar
½ cup margarine
1⅓ cup sifted whole wheat flour

Second part:
2 eggs
½ cup honey or corn syrup
1 tsp. vanilla
2 tbsp. flour
½ tsp. salt
1 cup coconut
¾ cup nuts

Blend first part and pat evenly into greased 9-inch-by-12-inch pan. Bake on middle rack of oven at 350°F for 10 minutes. Blend second part, adding nuts and coconut last, and spread on top of baked crust. Return to oven and continue baking for 20 minutes. Do not overbake.

CHEWY NOELS

2 tbsp. butter or margarine
2 eggs
1 cup brown sugar, firmly packed
5 tbsp. whole wheat flour

1 cup chopped nuts
1 tsp. vanilla extract
confectioners sugar

Melt butter in a 9-inch square pan. Remove from heat. Beat eggs slightly. Combine sugar, flour, and nuts and stir into beaten eggs. Add vanilla. Pour mixture over butter. Don't stir. Bake at 350°F for approximately 20 minutes. Turn out of pan onto rack, cut into oblongs, and dust bottom side with confectioners sugar. If desired, write "Noel" across top, using a white frosting. Makes 18.

COCONUT MACAROONS

½ cup honey
¼ tsp. almond flavoring

1 cup powdered milk, noninstant
1 cup or less fine coconut

Blend flavoring with honey. Add powdered milk and mix well, then add coconut and mix. Form small balls and flatten slightly. Place on buttered or Teflon cookie sheet. Put under broiler halfway down in the oven. Bake or broil for about 3 minutes or until golden brown. Cool before removing. Watch carefully. If non instant milk is not available, put instant milk into blender and run for a few minutes.

CAROB MACAROONS

Mix together:
3 cups uncooked oatmeal
4 tbsp. carob powder
1 cup coconut
½ cup sunflower seeds

Melt over heat:
2 cups raw sugar
½ cup milk
¼ lb. margarine
1 tbsp. vanilla
¼ tsp. salt

Add to dry mixture. Drop by teaspoonfuls onto cookie sheet. Bake 10 minutes at 350°F.

HENRIETTAS

1 square butter
1 cup raw sugar
2 egg yolks
1 cup sifted whole wheat flour

½ tsp. baking powder
1 tsp. vanilla
¼ tsp. salt

Cream butter and sugar until fluffy. Add egg yolks. Mix well. Gradually add flour, baking powder and salt. Beat well. Add vanilla. This makes a stiff dough. Press into 8-inch-by-9-inch pan. Spread with meringue made by beating 2 egg whites until stiff, then adding ½ cup brown sugar, and folding in 1 cup chopped pecans. Bake at 350°F for 30 to 35 minutes. Cut into squares.

BANANA OATMEAL CRISP

Cover teflon cookie sheet with a thin layer of oatmeal Blend or mash thoroughly 4 medium bananas and 4 tbsp. honey. Drizzle mixture over oatmeal and bake at 250°F until leathery, about 1 hour. Remove from pans; cut while warm and cool. If not crisp when cool, return to oven and continue baking at 200°F until crisp.

ICE BOX COOKIES

1 cup butter or margarine
2 cups brown sugar
3 eggs, beaten
1 tsp. vanilla
1 tsp. cream of tartar

1 tsp. soda
3¼ cups whole wheat flour
1 cup dates, chopped
1 cup nuts

Cream margarine, sugar, and eggs. Add vanilla and sifted dry ingredients. Fold in dates and nuts. Knead like bread, form into long rolls 3 inches in diameter. Place in refrigerator 4 to 5 hours. Cut thin and bake on cookie sheets at 375°F for 7 minutes.

LUSCIOUS APRICOT BARS

¾ cup dried apricots
½ cup soft butter
¼ cup brown sugar
1 cup sifted whole wheat flour
½ tsp. baking powder
½ tsp. salt

½ cup Kellogg's All Bran
1 cup brown sugar, packed
2 eggs, well beaten
½ tsp. vanilla
½ cup chopped walnuts or coconut
Confectioners' sugar (optional)

Cover apricots with 1 cup water; boil 10 minutes. Water should be absorbed. Cool and chop. Blend butter, ¼ cup brown sugar and ½cup of the flour until smooth. Stir in All Bran. Spread mixture in bottom of ungreased 9-inch-by-9-inch baking pan. Bake in moderate oven (350°F) 15-20 minutes. Remove from oven.

Meanwhile, sift together remaining ½ cup flour, baking powder and salt. Blend together brown sugar and eggs. Stir in sifted dry ingredients. Add vanilla, nuts and apricots; mix well. Spread over baked layer. Bake in 350°F oven about 20-25 minutes longer. Cool and cut into bars about 1 inch wide, 1½ inches long. Roll in confectioners' sugar (optional).

Variation: Any dried fruit can be used in place of apricots.

GERMAN COOKIES (NO LEAVENING)

2¼ cups brown sugar
4 eggs
2½ cups whole wheat flour

1 tsp. cinnamon
¼ tsp. cloves
1 cup nuts or raisins or dates

Beat together eggs and brown sugar. Sift dry ingredients and add, blending well. Stir in nuts. Spread in cake pan. Bake at 350°F for 15 to 20 minutes. Ice lightly if desired, or cut while warm and roll in powdered sugar.

RAISIN·FILLED OATMEAL COOKIES

Mix:
2 cups oatmeal
2 cups whole wheat flour
1 tsp. salt
1 tsp. soda

Combine:
1 cup brown or raw sugar
1 cup melted shortening
1 egg beaten
1 tsp. vanilla

Combine shortening mixture and flour mixture into dough. Divide into two parts. Cover bottom of baking pan with half of dough. Press. Spread filling over and cover with remaining dough crumbled on top. Bake at 350°F until brown for 15 to 20 min. Cool 15 minutes, cut into squares.

Filling:
Boil together:
2 cups chopped raisins

½ cup water
½ cup raw sugar or honey

Variations: Dried apricots, dates, or apples used in place of raisins for filling is good. 1 cup orange marmalade or apricot jam can be used as filling.

OATMEAL COOKIES (MOIST)

1½ cups brown sugar (or part honey
 ½ cup shortening
1½ cups oatmeal
2 eggs
1 tsp. soda dissolved in ¼ cup hot water

1½ cups whole wheat flour
½ tsp. salt
½ tsp. cinnamon
1 cup raisins boiled in small amount of water
(nuts if desired)

Mix shortening, sugar, and eggs thoroughly. Add oats, dry ingredients, and soda. Add raisins and nuts. Drop by teaspoonfuls on cookie sheet. Bake 350°F for 15 minutes.

POTATO PUFFS (NO FLOUR)

½ cup mashed potatoes
1 cup dry milk
2 tbsp. honey

½ tsp. vanilla
sesame seeds, almonds

Mix all ingredients together. Add more dry milk if necessary for stiff ball. Roll small balls in sesame seed, press almond on top. Bake 350°F for 15 minutes or until golden brown.

OATMEAL COOKIES (CRISP)

Mix:
2 cups shortening, part margarine
3 cups brown sugar

4 eggs
2 tbsp. hot water
2 tsp. vanilla

Add:
3 cups whole wheat flour sifted with 1 tsp. soda, 1 tsp. baking powder, 2 tsp. salt, 1 tsp. each cinnamon and nutmeg, 4 cups oatmeal, 1 cup nuts, 1 cup carob chips or sliced carob bars. Drop by teaspoonfuls on greased cookie sheet. Bake 375°F for 8 to 10 minutes.

COCONUT OATMEAL COOKIES

1 cup soft butter
2 eggs
1 cup coconut
1 cup chopped nuts
2 cups brown sugar
(or 1 cup brown sugar, 1 cup honey*)

2 cups quick rolled oats
2 cups fine whole wheat flour
1 tsp. baking powder
½ tsp. salt
1 tsp. soda

Cream butter and brown sugar, add eggs and beat. Add coconut, nuts, and rolled oats. Sift dry ingredients together and add to above. Drop by teaspoonfuls on lightly greased cookie sheet. Bake at 350°F about 10 minutes.

*Substituting honey for part of the sugar makes a flatter, chewier cookie, the texture of a macaroon.

DATE COOKIES (NO BAKE)

¾ cup raw or brown sugar
1 cup cut-up dates
2 well-beaten eggs
1 tsp. vanilla

1 cup each corn flakes and Rice Crispies or puffed wheat, puffed rice, or toasted millet
1 cup chopped nuts
2 oz. fine coconut

In heavy skillet mix sugar, eggs, and dates. Cook and stir over medium heat about 5 minutes or until mixture pulls away from pan. Cook 3 minutes longer, remove and add vanilla and nuts, then fold in cereals. Form in balls and roll in coconut.

FILLED DATE COOKIES

1 cup shortening
3 eggs
½ cup water
1 tsp. vanilla
3½ cups whole wheat flour

2 cups raw or brown sugar
½ tsp. salt
1 tsp. soda
⅓ tsp. cinnamon

Heat oven to 375°F. Mix thoroughly shortening, brown sugar, and eggs. Stir in water, vanilla. Sift and stir in flour, soda, salt, and cinnamon. Drop by teaspoonfuls onto greased cookie sheet. Place 1 tsp. filling on dough, cover with 1 tsp. dough. Bake 10 minutes or more.

Filling: Cook together until thick, stirring constantly, 2 cups dates (cut small) ¾ cup honey, ¾ cup water. Add ½ cup chopped nuts. Cool.

DATE PINWHEEL COOKIES

Dough:
¾ cup margarine
¼ cup oil
1 cup brown sugar
¾ cup honey
3 eggs, beaten

4 cups sifted whole wheat flour
1 tsp. salt
½ tsp. soda
1 tsp. baking powder
1 tsp. cinnamon

Cream margarine, oil, sugar, add eggs. Add rest of ingredients and blend well. Chill. Roll dough ¼-inch thick on wax paper. Spread with filling. Roll up like jelly roll Chill. Slice ¼ inch thick. (Hint: If dough mashes when slicing, butter a string, bring under roll, cross, and pull) Bake 10 to 12 minutes at 350°F.

Filling:
2¼ cups cut-up dates
½ cup honey
1 cup water

1 cup chopped nuts
2 tsp. lemon juice

Cook dates, honey, and water until thick. Add nuts and lemon juice and chill. Spread on dough.

DATE BARS

¾ cup shortening
1 cup brown sugar
1¾ cup whole wheat flour
½ tsp. soda
1 tsp. salt
1½ cup rolled oats

Filling:
3 scant cups cut-up dates
¼ cup brown sugar
1½ cup water

Mix shortening and sugar. Add dry ingredients. Sprinkle half of mixture on bottom of 12-inch-by-12-inch pan. Press down. Cook filling ingredients over low heat for 10 minutes. Cool and spread over mixture. Spread remaining mixture on top. Bake 375°F for 25 minutes or less. Cut while warm.

DATE STICKS

1 cup whole wheat flour
1 cup brown sugar
2 cups dates, chopped
½ cup nuts
2 eggs, beaten

½ tsp. salt
1 tsp. baking powder
1 tbsp. melted butter
1 tbsp. hot water

Sift flour once, measure and add baking powder and salt. Sift again. Add sugar gradually to eggs. Add butter, dates, and nuts. Add flour alternately with hot water, beating well after each addition. Divide into 2 greased, 8-inch-by-8-inch-by-2-inch pans. Spread dough thin. Bake at 325°F for 30 to 35 minutes. Cool and cut in strips 3-inch-by-1-inch. Remove and roll in powdered sugar or dry regular powdered milk. Makes 2½ dozen.

DATE NUT ICE BOX COOKIES

2 cups raw or brown sugar
1 cup shortening
2 eggs beaten
1 tsp. soda dissolved in 2 tbsp of water

3½ cups whole wheat flour
½ tsp. baking powder
¾ tsp. salt.
1 lb. dates chopped (2½ cups)
1 cup chopped nuts

Cream shortening, sugar, add eggs, and soda. Add dry ingredients. Stir in dates and nuts. Form into rolls, cover with wax paper. Let stand overnight in refrigerator. When ready to use, slice ½-inch thick and bake 8 to 10 minutes. Bake at 350°F or 375°F.

FAVORITE RAISIN COOKIES (LIGHT)

2 cups raisins

1½ cups water

1 tsp. soda

1 cup shortening or 2 squares margarine

3 eggs

2 cups raw or brown sugar

½ tsp. salt

4 cups whole wheat flour

2 tsp. pumpkin pie spice

1 cup nuts

Boil raisins and water 5 minutes. Cool and add 1 tsp. soda. Blend sugar, shortening, and eggs. Beat well Add sifted dry ingredients and raisin mixture. Add nuts. Mix and drop by teaspoonfuls on greased cookie sheet. Bake at 375°F for 15 minutes.

BOILED RAISIN COOKIES

2 cups raisins

2 cups water

1 cup shortening

1 cup honey

2 eggs, beaten

3½ cups whole wheat flour

1 tsp. baking powder and 1 tsp. soda

1 tsp. cinnamon

½ tsp. cloves

½ tsp. salt

Boil raisins and water 10 minutes. Cool and add shortening, honey, and eggs. Sift together dry ingredients and add. Stir in nuts. Drop from teaspoon on greased cookie sheet. Bake 375°F for 10 to 15 minutes.

RAISIN FILLED COOKIES

1 cup raw sugar

½ cup shortening

1 egg

½ tsp. vanilla

½ tsp. salt

½ tsp. soda

2 cups whole wheat flour

¼ cup or less milk to help hold together

Form in rolls and chill overnight in refrigerator. Slice and fill.

Filling:

1 cup ground raisins

½ cup nuts, chopped

¼ cup raw or brown sugar

½ cup water

1 scant tbsp. flour

Cook until thickens. Add 1 tbsp. lemon juice. Place spoonful on slice of cookie dough and press another slice on top. Bake 350°F for 15 minutes.

CAROB BROWN SUGAR SQUARES

⅔ cup shortening
¾ cup brown sugar
3 eggs
2⅔ cup sifted whole wheat flour

2 tsp. baking powder
1 tsp. salt
1 cup nuts, chopped well
1 pkg. carob chips

Melt shortening, cool. Stir in brown sugar. Beat in eggs till smooth. Add dry ingredients and carob chips. Bake at 325°F in dripper pan for 30 minutes. When nearly cool, cut into squares.

BROWN SUGAR SQUARES (CHEWY)

1 egg, unbeaten
1 cup brown sugar, packed
1 tsp. vanilla
½ cup sifted whole wheat flour

¼ tsp. baking soda
¼ tsp. salt
1 cup coarsely chopped walnuts

Grease an 8-inch square pan. Stir together egg, vanilla, and sugar. Quickly stir in flour, soda, and salt. Add walnuts. Spread in pan and bake at 350°F for 18 to 20 minutes. (Should be soft in center when taken from oven). Cool in pan and cut into squares.

ORANGE DROP COOKIES

¾ cup honey
¾ cup shortening
1 egg
1½ cup cooked, mashed carrots
1 tsp. vanilla

2 cups whole wheat flour
1 tsp. baking powder
½ tsp. salt
1 cup chopped walnuts

Beat honey, shortening, and egg together. Add carrots and mix well. Sift dry ingredients and add to first mixture. Add vanilla and nuts. Mix well. Drop by teaspoonfuls on greased cookie sheet. Bake 15 minutes at 375°F.

Frosting: Grated rind of ½ orange, pinch of salt, and juice of ½ orange. Add powdered sugar until of spreading consistency. Drizzle over slightly warm cookies.

CAROB CHIP COOKIES

½ cup shortening
¾ cup brown sugar
½ tsp. vanilla
1 egg, beaten
1 cup plus 2 tbsp. whole wheat flour

½ tsp. soda
½ tsp. salt
½ cup nuts
1 cup carob chips

Blend shortening, sugar, egg, vanilla. Sift dry ingredients together, add to shortening mixture and beat, then add nuts and chips. Drop by spoonfuls on greased cookie sheet. Bake 375°F for 10 minutes.

EASY FRUIT NUT BARS

¾ cup sifted whole wheat flour
1 cup brown sugar
¼ tsp. baking powder
⅓ tsp. salt
½ cup Mazola corn oil

2 eggs, unbeaten
½ tsp. vanilla
1 cup (8 oz. pkg.) finely cut dates
1 cup chopped nuts
1 heaping tbsp. apricot jam

Mix and sift first four ingredients into a bowl. Make a well and add in order: oil, eggs, and vanilla. Beat until smooth. Add dates, nuts and jam. Mix well. Turn into greased shallow baking (11-inch-by-7-inch-by-1½ inch) pan. Bake in moderate oven 350°F for 35 to 40 minutes. Cut into bars while warm. Dust with confectioners sugar. Makes 20 bars.

SPICED CARROT COOKIES

¾ cup shortening
¾ cup raw or brown sugar
1 egg
1 tsp. baking powder
1 tsp. vanilla
1½ cups cooked, mashed carrots

2 cups whole wheat flour
½ tsp. salt
1 tsp. cinnamon
½ tsp. cloves
½ tsp. nutmeg
1 cup chopped walnuts

Beat sugar, shortening, and egg together. Add carrots. Add sifted dry ingredients. Add nuts last. Drop from teaspoon onto greased cookie sheet and bake 375°F for 15 minutes. Frost if desired.

HAWAIIAN DROP COOKIES

2 cups whole wheat flour
2 tsp. baking powder extract
½ tsp. salt
⅔ cup shortening
1¼ cups brown sugar

1 egg
½ cup drained, crushed pineapple
½ cup shredded coconut, fine
½ tsp. each almond and vanilla
extract

Cream shortening, sugar, extracts; add egg. Beat until fluffy. Blend in pineapple and dry ingredients. Drop by teaspoonfuls on greased cookie sheet. Sprinkle with coconut. Bake in 325°F oven about 20 minutes. Store in Tupperware or other tight container.

FRUIT SQUARES (APPLE SAUCE OR MINCE MEAT)

Crust:
¼ cup brown sugar
3 tbsp. shortening
¼ cup milk

1½ tsp. baking powder
1½ cups whole wheat flour
½ tsp. salt

Mix shortening and sugar. Add milk and sifted dry ingredients. Roll out in two parts. Fit one piece in 8-inch-by-13-inch pan. Fill with apple sauce or mincemeat or raisin filling. Place remaining crust on top. Slash here and there. Bake 375°F for 25 minutes. Ice lightly with powdered sugar and water and few drops of vanilla or maple flavoring.

CHEWY CAROB CHIP COOKIES

½ cup shortening
½ cup butter
2 cups brown sugar
2 eggs, beaten
1 tsp. baking powder
1 tsp. cloves
2 tsp. nutmeg

2 cups apple sauce
2 cups quick cooking oats
2 cups chopped nuts
2 pkgs. (6 oz.) carob chips
1 tsp. salt
2 tsp. baking soda
3½ cups whole wheat flour

Cream shortening and butter together. Add sugar and blend well. Stir in eggs and mix well. Sift dry ingredients and add alternately with apple sauce. Stir in oats, chopped nuts, and carob chips. Drop by teaspoons onto greased baking sheet. Bake 12 to 15 minutes in 375°F oven. May be frozen.

MOLASSES COCONUT LUNCH BOX BARS

3 eggs
½ cup honey
½ cup light molasses
⅔ cup butter or margarine, melted
2 cups sifted whole wheat flour
½ tsp. salt
½ tsp. baking soda

½ tsp. cinnamon
½ tsp. nutmeg
¼ tsp. ground cloves
¼ tsp. mace
1 can (4 oz.) flaked coconut
1 cup raisins

Beat eggs with honey until well mixed. Gradually beat in molasses and melted butter. Mix and sift flour, salt, baking soda, and spices; blend into molasses mixture. Stir in coconut and raisins. Turn into greased 15½-inch-by-10½-inch-by-1-inch jelly roll pan. Bake at 350°F for 15 minutes, or until cake tester inserted in center comes out clean. Cool. If desired, cover with glaze and sprinkle with coconut, chopped nuts, toasted coconut, etc. Cut into 36 bars.

Glaze: While still warm, spread 3 tbsp. of honey over bars and sprinkle as above.

CARAMEL MERINGUE BARS

¾ cup margarine
1 cup brown sugar
3 eggs separated
1 tsp. vanilla
2 cups sifted whole wheat flour
1 tsp. baking powder

¼ tsp. soda
¼ tsp. salt
6 oz. (1 cup) carob chips
1 cup coconut
¾ cup chopped nuts
½ cup brown sugar

Blend margarine and sugar. Add egg yokes and beat 2 minutes. Add vanilla. Sift dry ingredients. Mix all together well. Spread dough evenly in greased 9-inch-by-13-inch pan. Sprinkle nuts, chips, and coconut on top. Press in. Beat egg whites until stiff. Add ½ cup brown sugar. Spread on top. Bake 350°F for 20 to 30 minutes.

BROWNIES (LIKE CAKE, NO LEAVENING)

2 cups brown sugar or 1 cup sugar and
1 cup honey
2 squares margarine
4 eggs
1¾ cup whole wheat flour

½ tsp. salt
6 tbsp. carob powder
1½ tsp. vanilla
1 cup walnuts or raisins

Cream margarine. Add sugar and honey, then eggs. Beat well. Add remaining ingredients and beat well. Pour into 9-inch-by-14-inch pan, greased and floured. Bake at 350°F 30 minutes. Ice if desired with Carob Frosting (see page 65).

DATE PENOCHE SURPRISE

⅔ cup shortening
1 cup raw sugar
1 egg plus 1 yolk
1½ cups sifted whole wheat flour
1 tsp. baking powder

½ tsp. salt
2 tbsp. milk
½ tsp. vanilla
½ tsp. lemon juice
1 cup cut-up dates

Cream shortening and sugar. Add eggs. Add dry ingredients, milk, vanilla, and lemon juice. Add dates. Mix well. Press into 8-inch-by-13-inch pan. Add topping. Bake 350°F for 50 minutes. Cut in squares when cool.

Topping: 1 egg white, beaten. Add ½ cup raw sugar, ⅔ cup nuts, vanilla.

BANANA NUGGET COOKIES

¾ cup shortening
1 cup brown sugar
3 bananas, mashed
1 egg
1 tsp. salt

1¼ cups rolled oats
¾ tsp. cinnamon
1½ cups whole wheat flour
½ tsp. soda
1 cup carob bits

Cream shortening and sugar until fluffy. Add banana and egg. Blend well. Sift flour, cinnamon, and salt together. Add to banana mixture along with rolled oats. Stir in carob bits. Drop from spoon onto greased baking sheet. Bake 350°F for 12 to 15 minutes. Makes 2½ dozen cookies.

WAIKIKI BANANA BARS (CHEWY)

¼ cup shortening
1 cup brown or raw sugar
½ tsp. vanilla
1½ cup whole wheat flour
1 cup mashed ripe bananas

1½ tsp. baking powder
½ tsp. salt
½ cup nuts, raisins or both
⅓ cup powdered sugar
1 tsp. cinnamon

Combine shortening, sugar, flavorings, and mashed banana in bowl. Sift flour with baking powder and salt. Add to first mixture. Mix well. Stir in nuts or fruit. Bake in 11-inch-by-7-inch pan 350°F for 30 to 35 minutes or until done. While warm, cut into bars and roll in powdered sugar and cinnamon. For lighter bars, add one egg.

HONEY (OR MOLASSES) SQUARES

Stir together:
½ cup oil
1½ cup brown sugar
2 eggs
½ cup honey (or molasses)
1 tsp. vanilla
½ tsp. salt

Mix in:
2 cups whole wheat flour
2 tsp. baking powder

Spread batter on large, greased cookie sheet with sides (at least 12-inch-by-18-inch), or 2 oblong cake pans. Bake 350°F 15 to 20 minutes. Cut into squares and remove from pan while still warm.

Variations: Add 1 cup chopped raisins, dates, or nuts.

RANCHO VERDE BARS

1 cup water
1 cup raisins
¾ cups honey
⅓ cup shortening

1 large grated carrot (1½ cups, packed)
1 tsp. each cinnamon, nutmeg, and soda
2 cups whole wheat flour
½ tsp. salt

Cook raisins and water until raisins are soft. Cream together honey and shortening. Add grated carrot and stir. Then add sifted dry ingredients along with raisins and water mixture. Add nuts if desired. Spread into greased 9-inch-by-12-inch pan. Bake 350°F for 25 to 30 minutes. Frost with 1 cup powdered sugar, ½ cup regular dry milk, ½ tsp. vanilla and milk to thin consistency. Makes 2 dozen 2-inch-by-2-inch bars.

RAISIN WHOOPEE COOKIES

1 cup seedless raisins
1 cup shredded coconut
1 cup whole wheat flakes
1 cup quick cooking oats
2½ cups whole wheat flour
½ tsp. baking powder
½ tsp. soda

½ tsp. salt
¾ cup soft shortening
¾ cup brown sugar (packed)
¾ cup honey
2 eggs
1 tsp. vanilla

Mix raisins with coconut, cereal flakes, oats, whole wheat flour, baking powder, soda, and salt. Beat shortening with sugar and honey. Beat in eggs and vanilla. Add dry ingredients, working with hands to form firm dough. Shape into large balls and place on lightly greased baking sheet. Flatten with palm of hand. Bake in moderately hot oven 375°F for 10 to 12 minutes. Remove cookies to cooling rack. Makes 2 dozen.

FROSTY HERMITS

1 cup All Bran
½ cup milk
1 cup whole wheat flour
½ tsp. baking soda
½ tsp. cinnamon
¼ tsp. nutmeg
¼ tsp. ginger

1 cup brown or raw sugar
½ cup soft butter or margarine
2 eggs
1 tsp. vanilla
1 cup raisins
½ cup chopped nuts

Add milk to All Bran in small bowl and let stand until moisture is taken up. Sift flour, soda, and spices, set aside. Beat sugar and butter until fluffy. Add eggs, vanilla, and bran mixture. Beat well Add sifted dry ingredients. Stir until mixed. Stir in nuts and raisins. Drop by tablespoonfuls onto lightly greased baking sheet. Bake at 375°F about 12 minutes or until golden brown. Cool and frost.

Vanilla Frosting:
1½ cup powdered sugar or part dry milk   2 tbsp. butter
1 tsp. vanilla hermits when cool.   2 tbsp. milk

Mix all together and frost

GUMDROP RAISIN COOKIES

½ cup butter or margarine
⅓ cup brown sugar
1 egg
⅔ cup honey
1 tsp. lemon flavoring
3 cups sifted whole wheat flour

1 tsp. baking soda
1 tsp. salt
1 cup golden seedless raisins
½ cup very soft gumdrops, cut in small pieces

Cream butter with sugar, egg, honey, and flavoring. Sift dry ingredients and add to creamed mixture a little at a time, mixing well. Mix in raisins and gumdrops. Shape into sausage roll 3 inches in diameter. Chill overnight. Slice with sharp knife (if dough becomes soft, put back in refrigerator to chill). Bake on greased cookie sheet at 375°F for 8 to 10 minutes. Makes 18 large cookies.

HONEY CAROB CHIP COOKIES

1 cup honey
1 cup shortening
2 eggs
⅓ cup evaporated milk
2½ cups whole wheat flour

1 tsp. soda
½ tsp. salt
½ tsp. cinnamon
1 pkg. (6 oz.) carob chips
2 cups quick cooking oatmeal

Cream honey, shortening, and eggs together. Sift flour, soda, salt, and cinnamon. Add alternately with evaporated milk. Blend in oatmeal and carob chips. Drop by teaspoons onto greased cookie sheet and bake in 375°F oven for 8 to 10 minutes.

OLD-FASHIONED MOLASSES COOKIES (LIGHT)

¼ cup shortening
¼ cup butter

⅓ cup brown sugar

Cream above three ingredients together and add:
1 egg slightly beaten
½ cup molasses, mild

¼ cup milk

Sift together and add:
2 cups whole wheat flour
½ tsp. salt
½ tsp. ginger or cloves

1 tsp. cinnamon
1 tsp. baking soda

Drop by spoonfuls on cookie sheet and bake at 375°F about 10 minutes. Rolled cookies can be made by adding enough flour (½ cup) to handle. Frost if desired.

ANGEL'S THUMB PRINT COOKIES (NO LEAVENING)

½ cup margarine
¼ cup brown sugar (packed)
1 egg yolk
1 tsp. vanilla

1 cup sifted whole wheat flour
¼ tsp. salt
1 egg white, beaten slightly with fork
¾ cup finely chopped nuts

Cream together margarine, brown sugar, egg yolk, and vanilla. Sift together and stir in flour and salt. Roll into 1-inch balls. Dip balls into beaten egg whites and then into nuts. Place on ungreased cookie sheet. Bake 5 minutes at 375°F. Remove from oven and press thumb into each cookie. Bake 8 minutes longer. Cool, then place jelly or tinted frosting into thumb print.

PEANUT BUTTER COOKIES

½ cup shortening
1 cup brown sugar (packed)
1 egg, well beaten
½ cup peanut butter

2 tbsp. sour cream
1½ cups whole wheat flour, sifted
1 tsp. soda

Cream shortening and sugar. Add peanut butter and mix well. Add egg and sour cream. Sift together dry ingredients and add, beating well. Form in balls the size of marbles, place on greased cookie sheet. Press with a fork. Bake at 350°F about 10 minutes.

PUMPKIN COOKIES

½ cup brown sugar
½ cup honey
½ cup shortening
2 eggs
1 cup pumpkin
2 cups whole wheat flour
¼ tsp. salt

½ tsp. nutmeg
1 tsp. cinnamon
½ tsp. ginger
½ tsp. cloves
2 tsp. baking powder
1 cup chopped pecans

Blend shortening and sugar. Add honey, eggs, and pumpkin. Sift dry ingredients together and beat into mixture. Add nuts last and drop from teaspoon onto a greased cookie sheet. Bake at 350°F for 15 minutes.

HONEY COOKIES

½ cup chunky peanut butter
½ cup butter or shortening
1 cup honey
½ cup mashed banana (1 medium)
1 tsp. vanilla
1½ cups flour

1 tsp. soda
½ tsp. baking powder
½ tsp. salt
½ tsp. cinnamon
¼ tsp. nutmeg

Cream together peanut butter and shortening. Add mashed banana and honey and mix well. Add vanilla. Sift dry ingredients and fold into creamed mixture until well blended. Chill 1 to 2 hours and drop by teaspoonfuls on greased cookie sheets. Bake in 350°F oven for about 15 minutes. (Note: No eggs are needed.)

GREAT HONEY COOKIES

5 cups whole wheat flour
1 tsp. salt
1 tsp. baking powder
1 tsp. each cinnamon, ginger
½ tsp. each cloves, nutmeg
1 cup shortening

2 eggs
2 cups honey
1 cup 7-Up or any plain, carbonated beverage
1 tsp. vanilla

Sift dry ingredients together until light and fluffy. Combine eggs, honey, shortening and vanilla. Beat well. Add carbonated beverage alternately with dry ingredients. Chill dough. Roll out and cut with glass or roll in balls and flatten slightly. Bake 8 to 10 minutes at 375°F if rolled or 15 minutes if in balls.

Variations: Add raisins or dates or coconut or while warm roll in powdered sugar and cinnamon or before baking form into balls and roll in fine coconut.

FRUIT BARS

¾ cup sifted whole wheat flour
⅓ cup butter
2 eggs, beaten
1 cup brown sugar
¾ cup chopped dates or ¾ cup coconut
1½ cups chopped nuts

⅛ tsp. baking powder
½ tsp. vanilla
½ tsp. grated lemon rind
2 tbsp. lemon juice
¾ cup powdered sugar or noninstant powdered milk

Mix flour and butter as for pastry. Sprinkle in bottom of baking pan. Bake 350°F for 10 minutes. Beat eggs, add brown sugar, dates, nuts, baking powder, and vanilla. Spread over dry mixture and bake 20 minutes more. Glaze with rind, juice, and powdered sugar while hot. Cool and cut into squares.

SWEDISH FRUIT BARS

1 cup brown sugar
½ cup butter
2 eggs
1 tbsp. orange juice
1 tsp. vanilla

1 tsp. soda
1 tsp. cream of tartar
2 cups whole wheat flour
½ cup each raisins and fruit cake mix

Cream brown sugar and butter. Add eggs, orange juice, and vanilla. Sift dry ingredients and add to above. Fold in raisins and fruit mix. Flatten in greased 12-inch-by-15-inch cake pan. Bake 350°F about 30 minutes. Mark in lengthened strips, 2-inches wide, while warm. Cool and roll in very thin powdered sugar frosting or warm honey, then in chopped nuts and coconut if desired.

PRUNE COOKIES

1 cup raw or brown sugar
2½ cups whole wheat flour
1 egg
1 cup shortening
1 cup prunes, cooked and cut fine

2 tsp. baking powder
1 tsp. vanilla
1 tsp. cloves
1 tsp. vanilla
1 tsp. soda

Combine sugar, shortening, egg, prunes, and vanilla. Sift dry ingredients. Add. Mix well and drop off teaspoon and bake 350°F about 15 minutes.

CONGO BARS (CHEWY)

2¼ cups whole wheat flour
½ tsp. salt
2½ cups brown sugar
1 cup broken nut meats
1½ cups (or less) carob chips

2½ tsp. baking powder
⅔ cup shortening
3 eggs
1 tsp. vanilla

Mix and sift flour, baking powder, and salt. Melt shortening and add brown sugar; beat until well mixed and creamy. Cool slightly. Add eggs, one at a time, beating after each addition. Add dry ingredients, vanilla, and nuts. Turn into 10-inch-by-15-inch pan and bake at 350°F for about 25 minutes. When almost cool, cut into finger length bars. Makes 3 dozen.

RAW APPLE COOKIES

1 cup brown sugar
½ cup shortening
½ tsp. vanilla
2 eggs
2 cups sifted whole wheat flour

2 tsp. baking powder
1½ tsp. cinnamon
½ tsp. allspice
1½ cups finely chopped apple
1 cup chopped raisins and nuts mixed

Cream shortening and sugar. Add eggs and vanilla and beat well. Add apples and mix well. Sift dry ingredients together and add, beating well by hand. Add raisins and nuts last. Drop by teaspoonfuls onto a greased cookie sheet. Bake 350°F for about 15 minutes.

COOKED WHEAT COOKIES (NO FLOUR)

4 cups cooked whole wheat, ground
1 cup dates or raisins ground
2 tbsp. butter
½ cup honey

½ tsp. vanilla
½ tsp. salt
1 cup nuts, chopped fine

Put wheat through meat grinder using finest blade to break kernel down completely. Mix honey and butter well. Add remaining ingredients and form into balls. Flatten to about ⅓inch thickness. Bake at 325°F to 350°F for 20-30 minutes. Cookies will be chewy.

TURKISH DELIGHTS (HIGH IN PROTEIN)

1 cup soy bean flour
1 cup dry regular milk

1 cup peanut butter

Moisten with 1 tbsp. lemon juice and 2 tbsp. honey. Mix well and roll or spread out on wax paper. Spread with filling, roll like jelly roll. Chill, slice ½-inch thick. Bake 350°F for 15 minutes.

Filling: 1 cup honey, 1 cup dry milk, ½ cup water. Cook in double boiler for 1 hour or until light brown. Add ½ cup chopped nuts and ground dates.

CAKES

HONEY SPONGE CAKE

1 cup honey
½ cup brown sugar
6 egg yolks
1¾ cup whole wheat flour,
sifted before measuring

⅓ cup orange juice
½ tsp. cloves
1 tsp. vanilla
6 egg whites
1 tsp. cream of tartar

Beat honey, sugar smooth. Add egg yolks one at a time and beat well until creamy and thick. Add orange juice, cloves, and vanilla. Add flour and beat well. Beat egg whites and cream of tartar until very stiff (for at least 5 minutes). Fold into above mixture. Bake in ungreased angel food pan at 325°F for 50 to 60 minutes or until cake springs back from touch. Remove from oven and turn upside down to cool 2 hours before removing from pan.

WHOLE WHEAT SPONGE CAKE

6 to 8 eggs, depending on size, separated
1½ cups raw or brown sugar
½ cup water
½ tsp. vanilla
½ tsp. lemon extract

¼ tsp. almond extract
1½ cups sifted whole wheat flour
¼ tsp. salt
1 tsp. cream of tartar

Beat with mixer yolks, sugar, water, and flavorings 5 to 7 minutes. Sift flour and salt 3 times. Add to egg mixture while continuing to beat. Beat egg whites and cream of tartar until very stiff, 5 minutes. Fold immediately into first mixture. Bake in ungreased angel food pan for 1 hour at 325°F to 350°F. Invert pan and allow to cool 2 hours before removing. This is an excellent cake for fruit toppings or lemon sauce and whipped cream. (Follow this recipe exactly as written.)

CAROB SPONGE CAKE

1 cup whole wheat flour, rounded
½ cup carob powder
½ tsp. salt
1½ cups brown sugar
6 large eggs, separated

½ cup water
1 tsp. vanilla
½ tsp. almond flavoring
1 tsp. cream of tartar

Sift flour, carob powder, and salt together twice. Beat egg yolks, sugar, and water together for 7 minutes with electric beater. Mixture will be thick. Add sifted flour and carob gradually, continuing to beat with mixer. Beat egg whites and cream of tartar for at least 5 minutes, until stiff. Fold immediately into first mixture. Bake in ungreased angel food pan for 1 hour at 325°F to 350°F. Invert pan and cool two hours before removing. Delicious served with whipped cream or frosted lightly with carob frosting.

HONEY SPICE CAKE

½ cup shortening
1 cup honey
2 eggs
¾ cup buttermilk, sour milk, or yogurt
2½ cups whole wheat flour
1 tsp. soda
1 tsp. baking powder

½ tsp. salt
nuts (optional)
1 tsp. cinnamon
¼ tsp. cloves
¼ tsp. nutmeg
1 cup raisins that have been softened by soaking or cooking (no juice)

Beat shortening, honey, and eggs. Add buttermilk, mix well. Sift dry ingredients together, add, and mix well. Stir in floured raisins. Bake 350°F for 30 minutes or until done. Frost, if desired with Sour Cream Frosting.

SOUR CREAM FROSTING

2 cups brown sugar
½ cup sour cream

1 tbsp. margarine or butter
1 tsp. vanilla

Cook sugar and cream in saucepan until it can be gathered together (not quite to soft ball stage). Remove from heat and add butter and vanilla. Allow to stand until cold. Beat until it turns light and spread on cake.

CAROB (CHOCOLATE) CAKE

½ cup shortening
1½ cups brown sugar
½ tsp. salt
2 egg yolks
1 cup buttermilk or yogur
1 tsp. baking powder

1 tsp. soda
5 tbsp. carob powder
2 cups sifted whole wheat flour
1 tsp. vanilla
½ cup boiling water
2 egg whites, stiffly beaten

Cream shortening, sugar, salt, and egg yolks. Add buttermilk alternately with sifted dry ingredients. Add soda dissolved in hot water, and beat. Fold in beaten egg whites. Bake in 2 layer pans for 25 minutes at 350°F or in 8-inch-by-12-inch pan for 35 minutes or until done. Frost with Carob Frosting.

CAROB FROSTING

Cream 2 tbsp. butter with ¾ cup noninstant powdered milk. Add ⅓ cup carob powder. Mix well, then add ¼ cup honey, 4 tbsp. cream or canned milk and 1 tsp. vanilla. Beat until smooth and add hot water (2 or 3 tbsp.) to make it spreading consistency. This frosting should be just thick enough to stay on cake, as it sets up readily.

CAROB SOUR DOUGH CAKE

Mix and let ferment for 2-3 hours in a warm place until bubbly:

½ cup thick sour dough starter
1 cup water

1½ cups whole wheat flour
¼ cup nonfat dry milk

Cream:
½ cup shortening
¾ cup brown sugar
1 tsp. vanilla

½ tsp. salt
1½ tsp. soda
1 tsp. cinnamon

Add 2 eggs one at a time, beating well after each addition. Mix in separate bowl 9 level tbsp. carob powder and 6 tbsp. warm water. Add to above mixture. Combine with sour dough. Mix at low speed until blended. Bake in 2 layer pans or 1 large pan at 350°F for 25 to 30 minutes.

Cool and frost with Carob Frosting. This is like an old fashioned, dark chocolate cake. Very moist.

BOILED RAISIN APPLE SAUCE CAKE

2 cups apple sauce
2 cups honey
1 cup cold water
1 cup shortening

1 small pkg. seedless raisins
1 heaping tsp. cinnamon
1 tsp. nutmeg
1 tsp. cloves

Combine the above ingredients in pan and bring to a boil. Cook 5 minutes. Remove from heat and cool. Sift together 4 cups whole wheat flour, 2 rounded tsp. soda, and 1 tsp. salt. Add to cooled mixture. If desired add 1 cup nuts. Bake in dripper pan or loaf tin in 350°F oven for 1 hour, or until done. (This cake is delicious to use as base for fruit cake). Add 1½ cups fruit mix, dates, and extra nuts.

APPLE SAUCE CAKE

1 cup apple sauce
1 egg, beaten
½ cup shortening
1 cup brown sugar
1¾ cups whole wheat flour
1 tsp. baking powder
½ tsp. salt

1½ tsp. cinnamon
1 tsp. allspice
1 tsp. nutmeg
¼ tsp. cloves
1 cup raisins (cook raisins in small
amount of water)
nuts (optional)

Mix shortening, sugar, and egg. Add apple sauce. Sift together dry ingredients. Add to above mixture. Beat thoroughly. Add floured raisins and nuts. Bake 350°F for 45 to 50 minutes or until done. Frost with Brown Sugar Frosting if desired. (see page 68)

BOILED RAISIN CAKE

2 cups raisins
2 cups sugar, raw or brown
3 cups water
½ cup shortening
4 cups sifted whole wheat flour
2 tsp. cinnamon

1 tsp. cloves
1 tsp. allspice
1 tsp. nutmeg
2 tsp. soda
1 cup nuts

Boil raisins, sugar, and water for 10 minutes. Add shortening and cool. Add remaining ingredients. Bake in 8-inch-by-12-inch pan. Before baking add topping of ½ cup brown sugar and ½ cup carob chips. Bake 15 minutes at 375°F. Lower to 300°F for 45 minutes.

CHRISTMAS CAKE

Boil together 2 minutes:
1 cup water
1 cup brown sugar
1 cup raisins
½ cup butter
1 tbsp. carob powder
1 tsp. cinnamon

Cool then add:
1 tsp. soda
2 cups whole wheat flour
1 cup fruit mix and nuts

Mix well and bake in loaf tin 1 hour at 325°F or until toothpick comes out clean.

RAW APPLE CAKE

1 cup brown sugar
½ cup shortening
2 cups (sifted) whole wheat flour
1½ tbsp. carob powder
1½ cups grated raw apple or 2 cups (packed) depending on how juicy

1 tsp. salt
1 tsp. each cinnamon, nutmeg, allspice
2 tsp. soda
1 cup raisins or dates
½ cup nuts

Cream sugar and shortening, then add grated apple. Mix. Sift dry ingredients together. Add to above. Fold in floured raisins and nuts. Bake 325°F for 1 hour or until done. Toothpick inserted in center will come out clean. For a more moist cake, boil raisins or dates in small amount of water until water is cooked out.

BANANA CAKE

1 square butter
1 cup honey
2 cups whole wheat flour
1 tsp. baking soda
1 tbsp. sour milk

½ tsp. salt
1 tsp. cinnamon
3 ripe bananas, mashed
1 cup raisins, boiled in ½ cup water
2 eggs

Cream together butter and honey, add beaten eggs, bananas, raisins. Sift dry ingredients and add. Mix thoroughly. Bake in cake pan 35 minutes at 325°F or loaf tin at 325°F for 1 hour. Frost if desired.

BROWN SUGAR FROSTING

3 tbsp. butter
1½ cups brown sugar

½ cup canned milk
½ cup or more noninstant dry milk

Melt butter, add sugar, and stir until dissolved. Add canned milk and stir for about 1 minute. Remove from heat, cool, and add powdered milk. If necessary, add a little more milk.

DATE CAKE

½ cup soft margarine
1 cup brown sugar
2 eggs, beaten
2 tbsp. grated orange rind
3 tsp. baking powder
2 cups sifted whole wheat flour

½ tsp. salt
¾ cup sour milk
1 cup chopped dates softened in water
2 cup chopped nuts mixed with ¼ cup flour

Cream butter, sugar, and eggs until fluffy. Add rind. Sift dry ingredients together and add alternately with milk. Add floured nuts and dates. Bake in 9-inch-by-12-inch pan 350°F for 35 to 40 minutes.

Topping: While cake is baking, mix juice of 1 orange, 1 tbsp. grated rind, ½ cup honey. Allow to stand, stirring occasionally. When cake is baked and before removing from pan, pour orange mixture over and allow to cool, or frost with Brown Sugar Frosting

PRUNE CAKE

1 cup raw or brown sugar
½ cup shortening
2 eggs
2 cups sifted whole wheat flour
1cup finely chopped prunes cooked
(or baby prunes)

1½ tsp. baking powder
1 tsp. soda
¾ tsp. cloves
½ tsp. salt
½ cup sour milk
½ cup nuts

Cream sugar and shortening. Add eggs and prunes. Sift dry ingredients, add to creamed mixture alternately with milk. Add nuts. Beat well. Bake 350°F for 30 minutes.

TOPPING FOR PRUNE CAKE

⅔ cup brown sugar
¼ cup table cream
6 tbsp. melted butter

½ cup coconut
1 tsp. vanilla

Combine ingredients. Spread on warm cake. Place under broiler until bubbly.

SPICY CARROT CAKE

1 cup margarine
2 cups brown or raw sugar
4 eggs, beaten
1½ cups raw grated carrots
1 tsp. vanilla
2¼ cups whole wheat flour

4 tsp. baking powder
1 tsp. cinnamon
½ tsp. mace or nutmeg
½ tsp. salt
½ cup hot water

Mix first 5 ingredients, add sifted dry ingredients alternately with hot water. Bake 12-inch-by-8-inch pan, 350°F to 375°F for 30 to 35 minutes.

CARROT CAKE

2 cups whole wheat flour
2 cups brown sugar
1 cup cooking oil
⅓ cup water
2 tsp. soda

1 tsp. salt
2 tsp. cinnamon
3 cups grated uncooked carrots
4 large eggs

Mix dry ingredients. Add oil and water and stir well. Add eggs one at a time, beating after each addition. Add grated carrots. Pour into greased angel food pan or 8-inch-by-12-inch cake pan. Bake at 350°F for 45 minutes or longer.

Carrot Cake Icing:
½ box or 2 cups powdered sugar
4 oz. cream cheese, softened
½ stick butter

1 tsp. vanilla
nuts or coconut

Mix all together. If necessary add milk to spread.

ORANGE CAKE

1¼ cups brown sugar
½ cup butter or shortening
1 cup milk
1 tsp. vanilla
3 egg yolks
2 cups whole wheat flour

2 tsp. baking powder
½ tsp. salt
1 cup nuts
1 cup raisins
1 tbsp. grated orange rind
3 stiffly beaten egg whites

Blend sugar and shortening well, add milk, egg yolks, and vanilla. Sift together and add whole wheat flour, baking powder, and salt. Add nuts, raisins, and orange rind. Fold in stiffly beaten egg whites. Bake in cake pan 350°F for 30 minutes. Spoon Orange Topping over hot cake.

ORANGE TOPPING

1 tbsp. grated orange rind

½ cup honey dissolved in juice of 1 orange

Mix and spoon over cake as it comes out of oven

ORANGE PARTY CAKE (NO LEAVENING)

½ lb. butter or margarine
2 cups brown sugar
6 egg yolks, whites to be added later

2 cups sifted whole wheat flour grated
½ cup orange juice
rind of 2 oranges

Cream brown sugar and butter until fluffy. Add egg yolks one at a time, beating well after each addition. Add whole wheat flour, orange rind and juice. Beat thoroughly. Beat 6 egg whites until stiff and fold in. Bake in greased angel food or bundt pan at 300°F for 1 hour or until springs back from touch. This is a rich cake and needs very little topping. Good served with ice cream.

BROILED ICING

Mix ¾ stick margarine with 1 tbsp. canned milk or cream and ¾ cup brown sugar and boil 1 minute. Remove from heat, add 1 cup nuts, 1 cup coconut and pour over oatmeal cake and broil until golden brown.

OATMEAL CAKE

1 cup rolled oats
1½ cups hot water
1 cup brown sugar
½ cup honey
½ cup shortening
2 eggs

1½ cups sifted whole wheat flour
1 tsp. soda
½ tsp. salt
1 tsp. cinnamon
1 cup raisins

Pour hot water over oats and let stand. Cream sugar, honey, and shortening. Add eggs and beat. Add sifted flour with soda, salt, and cinnamon. Add oatmeal mixture and beat. Add raisins. Bake 350°F for 35 minutes. Top with Broiled Icing.

WHOLE WHEAT BANANA NUT CAKE

2 large bananas
¼ cup butter or margarine
1⅓ cups raw or brown sugar
¼ tsp. salt
2 eggs, separated

1 tsp. soda
2 tbsp. sour milk
2 cups sifted whole wheat flour
1 cup chopped walnuts

Mash and cream bananas. Add butter, sugar, salt, and egg yolks. Cream thoroughly. Dissolve soda in sour milk and add flour alternately with sour milk Stir in nuts. Mix well. Beat egg whites until stiff and fold into batter. Bake in greased and lightly floured 9-inch-by-12-inch baking pan or loaf tin at 350°F for 40 minutes or until done. Ice with favorite frosting or whipped cream. Orange topping is good.

PUMPKIN LOAF

3 cups brown sugar
4 eggs
1 small can (2 cups) pumpkin
1 cup oil
3⅓ cups sifted whole wheat flour
½ tsp. baking powder

2 tsp. soda
1 tsp. salt
1 tsp. cloves
1 tsp. nutmeg
1 tsp. cinnamon
1 cup chopped walnuts

Mix brown sugar and eggs, beat until fluffy. Add oil and pumpkin and beat thoroughly. Sift dry ingredients together twice and add, beating well. Add floured nuts. Bake in 2 long loaf pans. Bake at 325°F. for 1 hour 10 minutes or until done. Ice if desired. Include ½ cup pumpkin as part of liquid to make powdered sugar icing.

FILLED CUP CAKES

¼ cup butter or oil
⅔ cup brown sugar
1 egg
⅔ cup milk

1½ cups whole wheat flour
2 tsp. baking powder
⅓ tsp. salt

Cream butter, sugar and egg. Add milk alternately with dry ingredients.

Filling:
½ cup brown sugar
2 tsp. cinnamon
1 tbsp. whole wheat flour
¼ cup chopped nuts

2½ tbsp. melted butter
½ cup chopped dates or ½ cup chopped
raisins

Put small amount of batter in greased muffin tin. Add filling, add more batter and top with filling. Bake 20 to 25 minutes at 350°F to 375°F. Yields 12.

PIES

PIE-MAKING HINTS

1. Sift flour before measuring.

2. Use cold shortening and water.

3. Prevent bottom crust from being soaked with filling by spreading melted butter on bottom crust. Chill before adding cold filling.

4. For flakier crusts, chill single crusts or filled pies before baking.

5. With pastry brush, apply milk or egg white to top crust before baking, browns nicely.

6. Keep juices from boiling out by moistening edges of double crust pie before fluting.

7. Keep edges of crust from becoming too brown by cutting circles of brown paper and placing over edges of pie during the first 10 minutes of baking.

8. Flour for pies must be finely ground. To make a pastry flour, measure 2 cups flour then replace 2 tbsp. of flour with 2 tbsp. cornstarch. Sift together before using. Whole wheat pastry flour can be purchased at health food stores.

9. Whole wheat pie crust is more difficult to handle without tearing. Patch or pinch together.

VINEGAR PIE CRUST

2¾ cup whole wheat flour
¾ tsp. salt
1 cup Crisco or lard

1 egg
1 tbsp. vinegar
⅓ cup water

Blend shortening with flour and salt until size of peas. Beat egg, add ⅓ cup water and 1 tbsp. vinegar. Add to flour mixture and stir until it forms a ball.

Hint: Take 1 tsp. of egg mixture out and spread around on top crust before baking to give golden brown look. For two-crust pie, bake 450°F for 10 to 15 minutes, turn down to 350°F for another 30 minutes or more. For single crust bake at 450°F for 10 minutes.

NEVER-FAIL PIE CRUST

2 cups whole wheat flour
1 tsp. salt

5 tbsp. cold water
⅔ cup lard, cold

Sift flour and salt into large bowl. Remove ⅓ of this flour and make a paste by adding 5 tbsp. cold water. Blend lard with remaining flour until size of peas. Add paste and stir with heavy spoon until it forms a ball. Roll out and place in tins. Chill before baking. Makes 3 crusts. Bake 425° to 450°F for 15 minutes. Double crust pie: Bake 450°F 15 minutes. Then turn down to 350°F for another 30 minutes. For double crust pie, see hints 3, 4, 5, 6, and 8.

SPREAD-ON CRUST

2 cups fine or pastry whole wheat flour
½ cup vegetable shortening
1 tsp. salt

½ tsp. baking powder
½ cup water

With pastry cutter, blend flour, shortening, salt, and baking powder, reducing shortening to small bits. Add water and mix well. Spread on top of 1 large or 2 small deep dish pies. Bake at 350°F for 45 minutes.

PECAN PIE

3 eggs
1 cup honey
⅔ cup brown sugar

⅛ tsp. salt
½ tsp. vanilla
1 cup pecans

Beat eggs lightly. Add remaining ingredients. Pour into 9-inch unbaked pie shell. Bake 10 minutes at 400°F, then 40 minutes at 300°F.

DEEP DISH APPLE PIE

6 to 8 apples, tart
or add 1 tbsp. lemon juice
¾ cup honey
1 tsp. cinnamon

1½ tbsp. minute tapioca
2 tbsp. butter
1½ cups water

Fill baking dish to top with sliced apples. Drizzle honey between layers and sprinkle lightly with cinnamon and tapioca. Dot with butter. Pour 1½ cups water over all and put a layer of Spread-On Crust over top.

Variation: Any fresh fruit can be used the same way, eliminate cinnamon if desired.

PUMPKIN PIE (FOR UNBAKED SHELL)

1½ cups pumpkin
½ tsp. cinnamon
¼ tsp. ginger
½ tsp. nutmeg

½ tsp. salt
¾ cup brown sugar
2 eggs, beaten
2 tbsp. melted butter

Mix together, add 1½ cups scalded milk. Line a 9-inch pie pan with whole wheat crust (see hint on page 73). Bake 450°F 10 minutes. Reduce heat to 350°F and bake 30 minutes longer.

PUMPKIN CHIFFON PIE

1½ cups canned pumpkin
3 egg yolks
1⅓ tbsp. gelatin
½ cup milk
½ tsp. ginger

¾ tsp. cinnamon
½ tsp. nutmeg
1 cup brown sugar or honey
whites of three eggs
¼ cup cold water

Stir together the pumpkin, egg yolks, sugar, milk, and spices. Cook in double boiler until custard like. Dissolve gelatin in cold water and let stand a few minutes. Add this to hot pumpkin mixture and stir well. Cool and when mixture starts to set, fold in egg whites, well beaten. Put in refrigerator and serve with whipped cream or Honey Meringue.

PUMPKIN PIE (FOR BAKED SHELL)

Mix:

⅓ cup cornstarch
¾ cup honey
½ tsp. cinnamon
½ tsp. ginger

½ tsp. nutmeg
2 cups scalded milk
2 egg yolks
1½ cups pumpkin

Blend first 5 ingredients with 2 cups scalded milk. Stir constantly until thickened. Cook 10 minutes. Add 2 egg yolks. Stir and cook 1 minute. Add 1½ cups pumpkin. Remove and cool. Fill cooked pie shell and cover with cream.

PUMPKIN PECAN PIE

3 slightly beaten eggs
1 cup pumpkin
1 cup brown sugar or 1 cup honey
½ cup dark Karo syrup

½ tsp. cinnamon
¼ tsp. salt
1 cup chopped pecans

Combine first 6 ingredients. Pour into unbaked pastry shell. Top with nuts. Bake 350°F for 40 minutes.

SODA CRACKER PIE

12 soda crackers, coarsely crushed
1 cup walnuts
1 cup brown sugar

3 egg whites
1 tsp. baking powder

Beat egg whites until stiff. Add 1 cup sugar slowly, plus 1 tsp. baking powder and 1 tsp. vanilla. Add soda crackers and nuts. Grease 9-inch pie plate, spread mixture on. Bake 350°F for 30 minutes. Cool thoroughly and cover with ½ pint whipping cream, whipped and sweetened. Grate carob coating on top if desired. Let stand 5 or more hours before using.

*Several varieties of whole wheat snack crackers are available at health food stores. 1 cup dry whole wheat bread crumbs can be substituted for soda crackers.

BLUEBERRY TARTS

1 recipe Vinegar Pie Crust (see page 74). Roll out and cut in circles and place in muffin tins. Prick well Bake until lightly brown at 425°F for about 10 minutes. Makes about 50 tarts. Thicken canned blueberries slightly. Add apple sauce to make berries go further. Fill tarts and top with whipped cream, sweetened and flavored with ½ tsp. lemon extract.

HONEY MERINGUE

1 egg white
¼ cup liquid honey

⅛ tsp. salt
½ tsp. vanilla

Beat egg white and salt in a small bowl until frothy. Drizzle honey in while continuing to beat. Add vanilla and beat until stiff. If used on top of a pie, bake at 300°F for 15 minutes. For large pie, double the recipe. For a gingerbread or cake topping, add 2 tbsp. of melted butter to 1 cup of meringue. Do not bake. Any leftover meringue can be stored in refrigerator and beaten again before using.

CARROT PIE

Mix together:
1⅓ cup honey
2 tbsp. flour
2½ tsp. pumpkin pie spice or
2 tsp. cinnamon and 1 tsp. ginger

Add:
2 cups cooked carrots that have been mashed well (done in blender or ricer)
1 cup canned milk
3 eggs
1 cup water, or carrot juice left over from cooking

Pour into unbaked pie shells, 2 small or one large. Bake at 400°F for 40 to 45 minutes. See hint number 7 on page 73.

LEMON CHIFFON PIE

1½ cups water
½ cup lemon juice
1 cup honey
½ square butter
⅛ tsp. salt

4 tbsp. cornstarch in ½ cup water
3 eggs separated
½ cup honey for whites
¼ tsp. lemon flavoring

Boil water, honey, lemon juice, salt, and butter. Mix the cornstarch and ½ cup water and stir into boiling mixture and cook for 2 minutes over direct heat. Have ready three well-beaten egg yolks. Pour part of the filling mixture over egg yolks. Then add this to the balance of the boiling mixture. Take off stove and fold the hot filling into 3 egg whites that have been stiffly beaten with honey, salt, and lemon extract. Cool, pour into pie shell and top with whipped cream or meringue.

SWEET BREADS

BASIC SWEET DOUGH (WHOLE WHEAT)

1 cake compressed yeast or 1 tbsp. dry yeast
1 cup milk
2 eggs
1 tsp. salt

⅓ cup brown sugar
¼ cup shortening
4 cups (about) sifted flour
(Fine whole wheat)

Dissolve yeast in milk that has been scalded and cooled to lukewarm. Add eggs, salt, sugar, shortening, and 2 cups flour. Beat until it springs back from spoon, add more flour. Mix well and turn out on lightly floured board. Knead until smooth and elastic, or until bubbles form on smooth side.

Place in a greased bowl, covered with a damp towel, and in a warm place (85°F to 90°F). Let rise until double in bulk. Dough can be shaped after one rising, or punched down for second rising. Turn out on lightly floured board or cloth and shape into desired roll shapes. Bake rolls without filling at 400°F for 8 to 10 minutes. Filled rolls should be baked at 350°F for 25 to 30 minutes.

CINNAMON ROLLS

1 recipe basic sweet dough
¼ cup melted butter
½ cup brown sugar

2 tsp. cinnamon
1 cup raisins or more - softened

Spread dough out on board, brush with butter, sprinkle with cinnamon, brown sugar, and raisins. Roll up and slice 1 inch thick by bringing a buttered string under roll, cross and pull. Bake at 350°F for 25-30 minutes.

FRENCH CHRISTMAS LACE

Make Basic Sweet Dough. Let rise twice and during second rising prepare the filling.

Boil together for one minute:

2 cups apples, finely chopped	½ tsp. salt
1 cup raisins, ground	½ tsp. ground cinnamon
1 cup dark brown sugar, firmly packed	

Cool. Then roll out dough into 14-inch-by-8-inch rectangle. Gently transfer to greased cookie sheet. Spread filling down center in strip about 4 inches wide. At each side of filling make cuts 2 inches long into dough. This makes 7 strips on each side. Cross alternate strips across center of filled section. On last strips, tuck under and seal. Cover with damp cloth and let rise until double in bulk. Bake 30 to 35 minutes at 350"F.

CROWN ROLLS

½ recipe of Basic Sweet Dough	½ cup nuts, finely chopped
¼ cup melted shortening	pecan halves
¾ cup brown sugar, firmly packed	seedless raisins
1 tsp. cinnamon, ground	

Use half a recipe or more of Basic Sweet Dough (see page 79). When dough is double in bulk, punch down.

Shape dough into walnut-size balls. Dip balls in melted shortening and roll in mixture of brown sugar, cinnamon, and chopped nuts. Arrange layer of balls in greased 9-inch tube pan. Sprinkle with pecan halves and raisins. Add another layer of balls and sprinkle with more halves of pecans. Cover with damp cloth and let rise to rim of pan, about 40 to 50 minutes.

Bake at 350°F until browned, about 35 minutes. Turn out of pan immediately and cool on cake rack. Serve hot or cold.

BANANA NUT BREAD

⅓ cup shortening	½ tsp. soda
½ cup honey	½ tsp. salt
2 eggs	1 cup crushed bananas
1¾ cups whole wheat flour	½ cup nuts
1 tsp. baking powder	

Mix in order given and bake 350°F for 40 to 45 minutes.

DATE NUT FILLING FOR ROLLS

1⅓ cup pitted dates, finely cut

½ cup brown sugar

½ cup water

⅓ cup walnuts, chopped

Add water, sugar and dates. Cook over low heat until completely blended and thickened. Add nuts. Cool. Use as spread on rolled dough.

GLAZES

To glaze the top of breads or rolls, use either the egg white or yolk with a teaspoon of water added. The whole egg may be beaten slightly and used also. Use a pastry brush to apply before the bread is baked.

WHOLE WHEAT SWEET BREADS (YEAST)

1 egg beaten

1 cup milk

1½ cups hot water

1½ pkg. or 1½ tbsp. dry yeast dissolved in ½ cup water

¾ cup honey

1 tbsp. salt

5 tbsp. cooking oil

7 cups whole wheat flour (about)

Mix together in large bowl egg, milk, honey, salt, hot water, and oil. Add 3 cups flour and beat until smooth. Add yeast mixture and stir in. Add flour to form a soft dough that is easy to handle. Knead 10 minutes. Form into a ball and let stand 20 minutes for easy handling. At this stage add fruits.

Variations: The following can be added to each loaf.

APPLE BREAD

Add:

1 cup finely chopped raw apples*

1 tsp. cinnamon

1 cup chopped walnuts

CARROT BREAD

Add:

1 cup finely grated carrots*

1 cup softened raisins

2 tsp. grated orange rind

*When apples or carrots are used, the added juices from them may make it necessary to add a little more flour. Whenever possible use oil when kneading.

DATE BREAD

Add:

1 cup cut-up walnuts	1 tsp. cinnamon
1 cup cut-up soft dates	

Divide in half. Shape. Put in greased pans (2) or cans (2-46 oz. cans, fill not quite half full). Let stand until almost double in bulk Not quite to top of cans or pans. Bake at 350°F for 30 minutes, then 325°F for 35 minutes. For added nutrition, 1 cup soy flour or 1 cup wheat germ may be added. When baking in cans, you will have a little dough left over with which to make scones.

ORANGE OAT TWISTS

1 cup milk, scalded	1 tbsp. dry yeast
1 cup rolled oats (quick)	¼ cup warm water
¼ cup margarine	1 tbsp. orange rind, grated
⅓ cup honey	1 egg beaten
1½ tsp. salt	3½ cups whole wheat flour

Pour hot milk over oats, stir in butter, honey, and salt. Cool to lukewarm. Stir in egg and yeast that has been dissolved in ¼ cup warm water. Stir in flour enough to make a soft dough. Knead until dough is smooth and elastic.

SWEET BREADS

Form into a ball and let rise in greased bowl until doubled in bulk Punch down and let rest for 10 minutes. Turn out on board and press into a rectangle 16-inches-by-8-inches. Cut in strips 4 inches long and 1 inch wide. Twist each strip and place on greased cookie sheet. Let rise until double in size. Bake 375°F for 15 minutes. Meanwhile, mix ¾ cup sugar and orange rind and let stand. Melt ½ cup margarine. Brush tops of hot twists with margarine and sprinkle sugar mixture over or dip twists into sugar mixture. Makes 32 twists.

Mixture to dip twists in after they are baked:

¾ cup brown or white sugar	½ cup margarine, melted
grated rind on one orange	

Variation: Blend orange rind with ½ cup honey. Cool twists before brushing on mixture.

ORANGE RAISIN BUBBLE RING

1 pkg. active dry yeast
¼ cup warm water
¼ cup butter
1 tsp. grated orange peel
¾ cup orange juice
¼ cup honey

1½ tsp. salt
1 egg, beaten
3½ cups sifted whole wheat flour
1 cup seedless raisins
Orange Sugar
2 tbsp. melted butter

Sprinkle yeast into warm water in warm bowl. Stir until dissolved. Melt ¼ cup butter. Add orange peel and juice and heat to lukewarm. Add honey, salt, and egg. Combine with yeast. Add about half the flour and beat until smooth. Gradually blend in remaining flour. Stir in raisins. Turn out onto floured board, and knead lightly about 1 minute, just until dough is smooth. Place in bowl. Brush top with additional melted butter. Cover closely and let rise in warm place until doubled in size (about 1 to 1½ hours). Punch down. Shape into 24 to 30 small balls. Melt 2 tbsp. butter. Dip balls in melted butter then roll in *Orange Sugar and arrange in layers in greased 9-inch tube pan. Let rise about 45 minutes to 1 hour, or until doubled. Bake at 350°F for about 1 hour until golden. Serve warm. Makes 1 large coffee cake.

*Orange Sugar: Mix 1 tbsp. grated orange peel with ½ cup brown sugar.

NUT BREAD

3 cups sifted whole wheat flour
4½ tsp. baking powder
¾ cups raw or brown sugar
⅔ tsp. salt

1 egg
1 cup chopped walnuts
2 tbsp. melted shortening

Sift flour, measure, and sift into bowl with baking powder, sugar, and salt. Beat egg. Add nuts, and shortening. Stir quickly and lightly into flour mixture. Pour into loaf tin or 46 oz. juice can and bake 350°F for 50 to 60 minutes or until done.

HOBO BREAD

3¾ cups raisins
1½ cups boiling water
1½ tsp. soda
4 thsp. butter
½ cup brown sugar

2 eggs
1¼ cups honey
1 tsp. vanilla
4 cups whole wheat flour
1 tsp. salt

Add boiling water to raisins and set aside to cool. Add soda. Cream butter, brown sugar, eggs, add honey and vanilla. Add whole wheat flour and salt with raisin mixture to above. Beat well. Bake in tall cans, greased and half filled, at 350°F for 45 minutes.

COTTAGE RAISIN BREAD

1 pkg. (1 tbsp.) active dry yeast
½ cup warm water
1 cup cottage cheese
1 tbsp. butter
2 tbsp. honey

2 eggs, beaten
¼ tsp. soda
1 tsp. salt
3 to 3½ cups whole wheat flour
1 cup raisins

Dissolve yeast in warm water. Combine warmed cottage cheese, butter, honey, beaten eggs, soda, salt, 2 cups flour and softened yeast. Beat with electric beater until dough climbs beaters. Add remaining flour to make a soft dough (you may not need all). Add softened raisins and knead well. Place dough in greased bowl and cover. Allow to rise until doubled. Punch down and form into loaf. Place in loaf and cover with damp towel. Let rise again until almost doubled. Bake 350°F for 45 minutes or until done.

LEMON BREAD

6 tbsp. butter
2 eggs
1 cup brown sugar
1 cup milk
2 cups whole wheat flour

1 tsp. (rounded) baking powder
½ tsp. salt
½ cup nuts
grated rind of one lemon

Cream butter and sugar. Add eggs and beat well. Add milk and dry ingredients alternately. Add lemon rind and nuts. Bake in loaf tin 325° F for 1 hour.

Topping: Mix juice of 1 lemon with ½ cup warm honey and spoon over hot loaf while still in pan.

PINEAPPLE BREAD

2 cups whole wheat flour
1 tsp. baking powder
½ tsp. salt
1 cup raisins
1 cup walnuts
1 egg

½ cup honey
2 tbsp. oil
1 tsp. vanilla
1 cup crushed pineapple
1 tsp. soda

Sift dry ingredients. Add raisins and nuts. Beat together egg, honey, oil, and vanilla. Add to flour mixture. Dissolve soda in pineapple and stir in well. Bake in loaf tin 350°F for 1 hour.

NUT AND FRUIT BREAD

2 cups sifted whole wheat flour
½ cup honey
1 cup chopped dates or raisins
½ cup chopped walnuts
1 egg, beaten
2 tbsp. melted shortening

1 cup crushed pineapple (not drained)
1 tsp. soda
1 tsp. vanilla
1 tsp. baking powder
½ tsp. salt

Sift flour, baking powder, and salt into bowl. Add dates and nuts. Combine honey, beaten egg, vanilla, shortening and add to flour. Dissolve soda in pineapple and add to above. Stir enough to blend. Pour in greased loaf tin. Bake 1 hour at 350°F. Add candied cherries if desired.

DATE BREAD

4 cups sifted whole wheat flour
2 cups raw sugar
1 tsp. salt
2 cups chopped dates
2 cups boiling water

2 tsp. soda
2 eggs
5 tbsp. melted butter
1 tbsp. vanilla
1 cup nuts

Pour boiling water over dates, add soda, butter, vanilla, brown sugar. Cool slightly and add beaten eggs. Stir flour and salt into above water mixture and mix well. Add nuts. Bake in 2 greased loaf tins or 2-46 oz. juice cans at 350°F for 1 to 1½ hours.

30-DAY BRAN MUFFINS

2 cups boiling water
1 cup margarine or shortening
1 cup brown sugar and 1 cup honey
4 eggs
1 quart buttermilk
2 cups 100 percent bran
(Kellogg's Bran Buds)

5 cups sifted whole wheat flour
1 tbsp. salt
5 tsp. baking soda
4 cups bran flakes
1½ cups dates or nuts, if desired, stirring into batter just before baking.

Pour boiling water over 100 percent bran and set aside to cool while mixing remaining ingredients. Cream together shortening and sugar, add eggs and blend well. Stir in buttermilk alternately with sifted dry ingredients, then stir in bran mixture and bran flakes. Bake 350°F for 20 minutes or until baked. Batter may be stored in covered container in refrigerator for as long as a month before using. Makes 5 to 6 dozen.

BLUEBERRY MUFFINS

1¾ cup whole wheat flour
1 tsp. salt
1 tsp. soda
2 tsp. cream of tartar

¼ cup honey or brown sugar
1 egg and milk to make 1 cup
⅓ cup melted shortening
1 cup blueberries

Break egg in a measuring cup and fill up to 1 cup with milk. Add honey and sifted dry ingredients. Add melted shortening. Mix lightly and fold in blueberries, drained. Bake in 12 greased muffin tins at 400°F for 20 to 30 minutes.

ORANGE HONEY MUFFINS

1 cup unsifted whole wheat flour
3 tsp. baking powder
½ tsp. salt
½ tsp. baking soda
1 cup rolled oats, uncooked
1 cup orange juice

⅓ cup honey
1 egg
3 tbsp. vegetable oil
1 tbsp. grated orange peel
raisins (optional)

Mix and sift flour, baking powder, salt, and baking soda. Stir in oats. Combine orange juice, honey, egg and oil. Beat until well blended. Add with grated peel. Stir just until all dry ingredients are mixed in. This batter is thinner than is usual for muffins. Fill well-greased muffin pans two-thirds full. Bake at 425°F for about 15 minutes or until golden brown. Makes 12 large muffins.

BEVERAGES, COCKTAILS AND SLUSHES

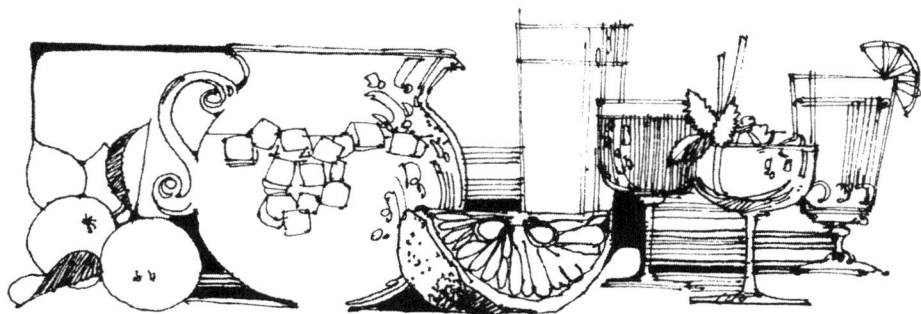

CRANBERRY PUNCH

1 lb. package cranberries
3 cups water
1½ 16-oz. cans frozen orange juice
½ pkg. raspberry jello

4 cups milk white honey
2 small cans frozen lemon juice or
2-4 oz. cans lemon concentrate

Boil cranberries and 3 cups water 15 minutes. Strain. Add water called for to dilute frozen juices according to directions. Dissolve jello in hot water. Add honey and dissolve before adding to juices. When using lemon concentrate add 10 cans water. Mix well together and add ice.

APRICOT-GRAPEFRUIT NECTAR

2 qts. apricots
2 cups water

1 46-oz. can honey-sweetened
 grapefruit juice

Put apricots through strainer to remove skins and strings. Add grapefruit juice and water. Pour over ice cubes.

APRICOT NECTAR VARIATIONS

Combine equal amounts of apricot nectar and pineapple or orange juice. Heighten flavor by adding small amounts of lemon juice and honey to taste. Pear, peach or grapefruit are good combinations with apricot nectar.

SPICED FRUIT DRINK

juice of 6 oranges
juice of 6 lemons
1-46 oz. can pineapple juice, unsweetened

5 qts. water
3 cups honey
2 sticks cinnamon, 1 tsp. cloves

Boil spices in 1 qt. of water and strain. Add other ingredients and heat.

SPICED GRAPE JUICE

1 stick cinnamon
¼ tsp. allspice
12 whole cloves
V2 tsp. ginger

¼ tsp. nutmeg
⅔ cup brown sugar
3 cups water

Simmer all ingredients ½ hour and let stand overnight. Strain and add ¼ cup lemon juice, 1 cup orange juice and 1 qt. grape juice. Serve hot.

SPICED CIDER AND FRUIT DRINK

1 gallon cider
2 qts. apricot and pineapple juice or cider and orange juice and apricot juice

Syrup:
2 cups water
4 sticks cinnamon
1 tsp. cloves

Boil syrup ½ hour and strain. Cool and combine with above juices and cider. Serve hot.

RASPBERRY LEMONADE

1 pkg. (10-oz.) frozen or 1½ cups fresh raspberries
½ cup honey
2 cans (6-oz. each) frozen lemonade concentrate, thawed and undiluted

ice cubes
fresh mint
1 bottle (32-oz.) lime and lemon carbonated drink (optional)

Combine raspberries, honey, and lemonade concentrate in a blender. Whirl until smooth. Pour mixture through a strainer to remove seeds. Pour into large pitcher and add carbonated water and ice cubes. Stir to blend.

STRAWBERRY PUNCH

1 cup washed and hulled strawberries
1½ cups milk

2 tbsp. honey
2 tbsp. undiluted frozen orange juice concentrate

Combine all ingredients in electric blender. Blend until smooth. Serve immediately. If desired, garnish with orange slices and strawberries. Serves 2.

BANANA ADE

Blend:
2 ripe bananas
2 cups orange juice

5 or 6 fresh pineapple chunks
(canned may be used)

TOMATO CONSOMME

Combine:
4 cups tomato juice
2 cans condensed consomme
4 whole cloves
8 peppercorns
½ bay leaf

½ tsp. salt
a little basil
1 small onion, chopped
a few celery tops
a few parsley sprigs

Simmer together 30 minutes. Strain. Reheat and serve garnished with diced avocado, buttered popcorn, croutons, chopped chives, or chopped green onion tops. Yields 6 cups.

TOMATO JUICE SPECIAL

1 No. 2 can tomato juice
3 tbsp. lemon juice
1 tsp. honey

¼ tsp. celery salt
1 tsp. worcestershire sauce

Combine ingredients and chill. Makes 5-4 oz. servings

FRESH FRUIT JUICES

With a juicer, any kind of fruit in season can be converted to a delicious beverage. Crisp apples, any berry, or grapes are the best.

MANNA

2 cups milk
1 banana
¼ cup raisins

½ tsp. vanilla
1 tbsp. honey

Blend well and drink.

FROSTED GRAPEFRUIT AND PINEAPPLE COCKTAIL

2 cups water
1 cup honey
1 can (16-oz.) grapefruit
1 can (16-oz.) crushed pineapple juice of
2 lemons

10 to 12 maraschino cherries, cut in
fourths
Carbonated lemon-lime beverage
(optional)

Make syrup of water and honey by boiling for 5 minutes. Cool. Beat grapefruit well to
break up sections. Add pineapple, lemon juice, syrup, and cherries. Freeze to mush. Fill
sherbet glasses one-half full. Add lemon-lime carbonated beverage to fill. Garnish with
a small piece of mint dipped in granulated sugar. Serves about 16.

PINEAPPLE GRAPEFRUIT COCKTAIL

1 can (16-oz.) grapefruit sections cut
into bite-size pieces
1 can (29-oz.) pineapple tidbits,or use
fresh pineapple

1 large banana, cubed
1 cup red grapes, seeded and cut in half
1 large orange, peeled and cut in small
pieces

Combine all fruit and allow to stand in refrigerator for several hours. Serve in sherbet
glasses topped with a maraschino cherry.

PINEAPPLE SLUSH

Freeze:
2½ cups crushed pineapple
3 bananas, mashed

2½ cups unsweetened grapefruit sections, fresh or canned

BANANA SLUSH

1 cup water
¾ cup honey
juice of 1 orange

juice of 1 lemon
2 bananas, mashed

Add hot water to honey and dissolve. Add remaining ingredients and freeze. When ready to use, spoon frozen mixture into cups. Add ginger ale and garnish with cherry.

GRAPEFRUIT SLUSH

1 can unsweetened pineapple
1 can unsweetened grapefruit

2 cups honey

Freeze, mash and add 7-Up.

FRUIT COCKTAIL SLUSH

1 can fruit cocktail
½ cup frozen orange juice

1 can 12 oz. 7-Up

Freeze half 7-Up, cocktail, and orange juice. Pour remaining 7-Up over. Add other fresh fruits if desired.

FRESH LEMON SHERBET

¾ cup honey
2 cups top milk, half-and-half, or canned milk

1 tbsp. grated lemon peel
⅓ cup lemon juice
green food coloring

Stir milk and honey together. Warm a little for easy blending. Add lemon peel and lemon juice, slowly stirring constantly. Color delicately with green food coloring. Pour into freezing tray with control at lowest point. When mixture is frozen, whip until light and creamy but not long enough to melt. Return quickly to freezing compartment and allow to finish freezing.

FROZEN GRAPES OR CHERRIES

Freeze seedless grapes or sweet cherries. Partially thaw before eating.

APRICOT FREEZE

6 cups (46 oz. can) apricot nectar*
2 cups pineapple juice
juice of 1 fresh lemon or orange

¾ cup water
¾ cup honey

Combine all ingredients and stir until honey dissolves. Freeze to a slush. Fill glasses two-thirds full, then fill with carbonated lemon or lime drink. Makes 12 to 14 servings

*Home-canned apricot nectar is made by putting fresh apricots through the blender, heating to boil with enough honey to sweeten, then canning.

ORANGE FRESH FRUIT FREEZE

Apricots, peaches, or pears are good. Puree any of these fresh fruits, sweeten slightly with honey and freeze. When ready to use, mix equal amounts of frozen puree and orange juice in a blender.

Variation: To 3 cups of freeze add ¼ cup dry powdered milk. A few pieces of pineapple added to the freeze is delicious.

QUICK FRUIT ICE CREAM

Peel and freeze bananas and strawberries. Put through juicer (Champion). Serve immediately. This is texture of soft ice cream.

Pineapple, pears, peaches or apricots alone or combined can be used the same way. If fruits are tart, add a little honey. Combinations such as pineapple and banana, pineapple and pear, or pineapple and apricot are good.

RUBY GRAPEFRUIT

4 large grapefruit
1 pkg. (10-oz.) frozen red raspberries

2 to 4 tablespoons honey (depending on tartness of grapefruit and your own sweetness preference)

Peel grapefruit, cutting deep enough to remove the white underlayer. Then extract sections by cutting close to the membrane on each side of the fruit wedge and carefully slipping out the whole section. Each grapefruit should deliver 11 beautiful sections. Squeeze the denuded membranes of any remaining juice into the bowl with the fruit. Heat raspberries until completely thawed, add honey. Then puree in an electric blender or food mill. Strain over grapefruit sections. Chill thoroughly and serve with pride. Makes 6 to 8 servings.

MISCELLANEOUS

FAMILIA

2 lb. old-fashioned rolled oats   1 lb. wheat germ
1 lb. raw sugar

Break up oats by rubbing through hands or put one-half of oats in blender for a few seconds. Combine ingredients and toast for 1½ hours, stirring every 15 minutes or so, about 325°F. Add ½ lb. broken filberts and ½ lb. broken almonds and ½ lb. rice polishings, toast ½ hour longer. Remove from oven and add 1 lb. large raisins. (Honey-dipped manuka raisins are good.)

CAKE CRUMB TOPPING

Use left-over molasses or any other cake. Dry out to grind into crumbs. Delicious on pudding, ice cream, or on cake frosting. Also good sprinkled on dry cereal.

CRAB TOMATO-JUICE SURPRISE

1 can (46-oz.) tomato juice   ½ cup lemon juice
1 cup crab, flaked   2 tbsp. honey
2 cups grapefruit pieces, canned or fresh   ½ cup catsup
     1 tsp. salt

Mix together and chill. Delicious.

HONEY BUTTER

½ cup butter   ¾ cup honey

Cream butter thoroughly. Add honey gradually and beat until fluffy. Place in refrigerator. Excellent on toast, rolls, pancakes, or waffles.

HONEY BUTTER (WITH EGG)

1 square butter or margarine   1 egg yolk
1 cup honey

Combine with electric beater until creamy and fluffy.

HONEY COCONUT SPREAD

Cream together   Add :
2 cups honey   1 tsp. coconut extract
4 tbsp. margarine   1 cup coconut

Use on hot rolls, scones or toast. Also good on warm cake, waffles or pancakes.

GRANOLA

7 cups rolled oats   1 tsp. salt
1 cup wheat germ   1 tsp. vanilla
1 cup raw or brown sugar   1 cup oil
2 cups coconut   1 cup soya flour
1 cup sesame seeds   grated rind of 1 lemon
¾ cup nuts, chopped

Bake in slow oven 200°F for 2 hours, stirring often. For chewier granola, substitute honey for sugar and bake only one hour. Add raisins or other dried fruits after baking.

CHEESE PUFFS

½ lb. grated nippy cheese   1 cup sifted whole wheat flour dash
½ cup butter   paprika

Combine cheese and butter, work in flour with paprika. Chill thoroughly. Shape into balls size of large marbles. Place on ungreased cookie sheet. Bake 450°F for 5 to 7 minutes. Serve warm.

FRENCH SALAD DRESSING

½ cup salad oil
⅓ cup vinegar
⅓ cup catsup
¼ cup honey

1 tsp. paprika
½ tsp. salt
½ medium onion grated
juice of ½ lemon

Mix together. Shake well prior to using.

YOGURT

2 qts. milk

8 tbsp. yogurt

Heat milk to boiling and cool to lukewarm. Stir in yogurt. Beat or blend in liquefier. Pour into containers and set in a pan of warm water. Keep adding hot water to keep it warm. It takes 3 to 4 hours to set. Refrigerate immediately. Eat plain or with fresh fruit, frozen or bottled. Apple sauce is especially good with it.

CLAM DIP

1 8-oz. pkg. cream cheese
2 tsp. lemon juice
1½ tsp. worcestershire sauce
3 or more tbsp. clam juice

½ tsp. salt
dash pepper
1 can (7 oz.) can minced clams, drained

Mix cream cheese with all ingredients except clams. Blend until smooth and add clams.

NOTES:

NOTES:

NOTES:

NOTES:

dri best

MINI RECIPE BOOK
AND
GENERAL DEHYDRATING INSTRUCTIONS

BY RUTH LAUGHLIN

Dehydrating is the finest food storage processing method known considering time, cost, longevity, nutritional retention and general storage benefits. One of the major advantages of dehydration is the storage space required. Because of the shrinkage, dehydrated foods require one-tenth of the space required of fresh foods.

Dehydrating has almost unlimited possibilities and is exciting and satisfying. It provides nutritional products and is very economical. You will be able to preserve surplus food. In the spring when dry onions and potatoes start to sprout it is a simple matter to dehydrate them for future use. A shameful amount of foods rots on the ground because people don't know how to preserve them or don't have the equipment. You can learn to experiment and enjoy creating your own dehydrated food specialties.

By preserving fruits in this manner you will be avoiding the use of so much sugar. In this country we consume 1/3 to 1/2 pound of sugar per day per capita. Sugar robs the body of B Vitamins, disrupts calcium metabolism, encourages tooth decay, disrupts white cell formation which leaves the body open to infections. Excess of refined carbohydrates have many disadvantages.

INSTRUCTIONS FOR USING A DEHYDRATOR OF YOUR CHOICE, IF INSTRUCTIONS ARE NOT INCLUDED.

1. Load trays from the bottom to the top. Fill 2 or 3 trays and turn on.

2. During humid weather set the thermostat up to 150° F. The normal setting   is 140° F.

3. Do not leave the dehydrator unattended for long periods of time unless you know the time required to dry the food inside.

4. Do not cover the vents.

5. Be sure to have a door or window open or a cross draft in the room during summer. During good weather set it outside. If cooler than 65° bring inside.

6. Coat trays very lightly with Pam on any tray inserts, or on the type of smooth, solid tray provided with your dehydrator, when drying sliced, juicy fruits, fruit leather and some vegetables such as zucchini and tomatoes, and remove while still warm.

PREPARATION PROCEDURES FOR DEHYDRATING FRUITS

Select fruit that is ripe or mature so that it will be at peak flavor. Fruit should be ripe but firm and as fresh as possible. Use very ripe, soft fruits for leathers.

If fruits are dried with controlled heat, air and humidity, it is not necessary to use sulfur or sodium sulfate to preserve color. Many people object to the taste that these products leave. A syrup* with ascorbic acid added will preserve color and provide a coating that will aid in Vitamin C retention in fruits such as peaches, apricots, pears and apples. You should slice fruit flat, not in a pie shape wedge as the thick side will take longer to dry. The thinner the slices the faster they dry. 1/8" to 1/4" thick is average for apples. Peeling apples,pears and peaches improves texture, appearance and speeds the drying process.

Place fruit on trays in a single layer not overlapping. Nylon net placed on the trays will prevent small pieces of foods that shrink a lot from going through the mesh. Diced carrots, shredded carrots, celery, peas, and rhubarb are examples.

Bananas tend to stick to trays unless they are sprayed with Pam or lightly oiled. Nylon net helps here, too.

STORING FOODS THAT ARE DRIED HARD
Remove food from dehydrator and let stand in open container 3 to 4 days to distribute any moist spots before storing.

HOW TO STORE FRUITS FOR A SOFT, PLIABLE TEXTURE

When fruit is rubbery and there are still moist spots it can be packed in clean canning glass jars. Cover jars with new lids and screw bands loosely. Set bottles in a pre-heated oven at 200° for 30 minutes to sterilize. Remove from oven, tighten bands and cool. When ready to use, fruit will be soft and pliable.

NOTE: If this method is not practical, completely dry fruit so that there are no moist spots left and store in odd jars or cans to keep free of dust. In humid climates it will be necessary to keep moisture out by using tighter lids. Store in a cool dark place. Temperatures of 65° F will result in only a 10% loss of vitamin C. Check food once a month for mold. If found, scrape or wash off and return to dehydrator.

To Shorten drying times turn the thermostat up to 160° for the first 2 hours then reduce to regular setting of 145° for remainder of the time.

To maintain good color in fruits such as apricots, dip in pineapple juice or I can frozen lemonade diluted with 1 can water.

SYRUP FOR DEHYDRATING FRUITS

2 cups water
1 cup honey or sweetening of your choice
2 tsp. Ascorbic acid powder (available near canning supplies) or juice of one large lemon.

Combine ingredients and warm enough to blend. Cool. Dip fruit in syrup and drain in colander before arranging on tray. Place cut sides up. This is a syrup and not only maintains color in the fruit but gives it a good sweet sour coating. You can use more or less according to taste or none at all for restricted diets.

AVERAGE DRYING TIME FOR FRUITS

PRODUCT	SIZE	TIME
Apples	1/4" slices	6-8 hours
Apricots	halves	20-24 hours
Bananas	1/4" slices	8-10 hours
Berries	whole-small	8-10 hours
Cherries*	pitted – blanched	12-20 hours
Grapes	whole – blanched	16-24 hours
Nectarines	slices	8-10 hours
Pears	slices	8-10 hours
Pears	small halves	16-20 hours
Peaches	slices	8-10 hours
Pineapple**	tidbit pieces or slices	20-24 hours
Plums (large)	halves	10-14 hours
Prunes	whole – blanched	20-24 hours
Rhubarb	1/2" pieces	8-10 hours

*Pitted Cherries can be dried whole. They will take about 26 hrs. If blanched they will take about 17 hrs. Seedless grapes will take 2 to 3 days. If blanched about 17 hrs. and will be a gold color.

**Place on nylon net covered trays.

There are many variables that influence drying times: moisture content of fruit, amount of fruit in the dehydrator, size of fruit, and humidity. You may turn the thermostat up to high for the first half of the drying cycle to speed drying time then turn temperature back down for remaining time. The temperature inside during the first part of the cycle while the fruit is giving up large amounts of moisture, will reach approximately 110°-125° as the fruit dries the temperature will climb. Temperatures under 140° F will preserve major enzymes which is important for fruits that are to be eaten raw.

TO DECREASE DRYING TIME OF PLUM AND/OR APRICOT HALVES
This is a helpful procedure, especially when the fruit is quite large. Press your thumb on the outside of the fruit half upwards to make the middle more even with the rest of the fruit before placing on trays, skin side down.

TESTS FOR DRYNESS

FRUITS	TEST	FRUITS	TEST
Apples	Pliable	Pineapple	Pliable
Apricots	Pliable to Hard	Prunes	Leathery
Bananas	Pliable	Grapes	Firm-chewey
Berries	Rattles	Nectarines	Pliable
Cherries	Leathery-Sticky	Peaches	Pliable
Raspberries	Hard	Rhubarb	Hard

DRIED FRUIT RECIPES

FRUIT LEATHER

Puree very ripe fruit in blender. Sweeten if desired. Pour out very thin, (about 2 1/2 cups per tray). Pour out on tray insert or on to a Seran plastic wrap that has been secured to trays with tape to prevent its curling over fruit. Bottled fruit can be used. Pour off some liquid before blending. Dry until puree is set. Peel off sheet while still warm. Add a natural oil flavoring to pick up flavor and color of such fruits as apple, pear or flat tasting apricots. Seran wrap can be placed directly on trays - will not melt.

All leathers should be dehydrated until the puree sets up and cannot be moved with finger pressure. Roll up with plastic wrap. An optional method is to pour puree out in six pancakes per tray. They will dry more evenly and much faster. If you are using leather for roll ups then dry in a sheet. Peel leather off and store in lighter plastic and reuse the heavier.

FRUIT SALAD LEATHER

1 quart unsweetened apple sauce
2 cups crushed pineapple
2 bananas
2 tbsp. orange flavoring

Puree in blender and spread 2 cups to a sheet on plastic wrap on cookie sheets or directly on trays.

FRUIT LEATHER ROLL UP

When using a dark colored fruit leather, a light filling is recommended to give contrast. Use the dark filling with light colored leathers.

Light Filling:
½ cup honey, room temperature
1 cup non instant dry milk
1 tbsp butter

½ tsp pure vanilla
½ to 1 cup coconut

Stir and knead enough milk and honey to make a soft mixture. Add remaining ingredients and spread out on fruit leather. Roll up tightly starting on longest edge. Cool before slicing.

Dark Filling:
½ cup dates, ground
½ cup raisins, coarsely ground
1 cup walnuts, coarsely ground
1 tbsp. lemon juice

1 ½ tbsp. honey
1 tbsp. peanut butter
1 tsp. finely grated orange rind (optional)

Mix all ingredients together and spread on leather. Roll up as above.

GRAPE LEATHER

After juice has been extracted from grapes, put pulp through a colander to remove seeds and skins. Sweeten to taste and spread out on seran wrap covered trays and dehydrate. Secure seran wrap to sides with scotch tape.

DANISH SWEET OR FRUIT SOUP

3 cups dried prunes soaked
½ cup minute tapioca
3 cups raisins
2 tsp. vanilla
1 cup dried apples

4 tbsp. butter
1 cup honey
2 sticks cinnamon or 1 tsp. ground cinnamon
⅓ tsp. salt

Cover fruit with water and boil until soft. Add honey, tapioca, vanilla and cinnamon. Add enough more water to make 1 1/2 quarts of liquid. Serve hot or cold. Use any dried fruit combination. Apricots and peaches are a good color combination.

DRIED FRUIT BALLS (TART)

1 cup raisins
1 cup dates
1 cup prunes

2 tsp lemon juice
1 cup figs
1 cup chopped walnuts

Optionally peaches or apricots are a good addition. Grind the dried fruit. I add chopped nuts and lemon juice. Form into small balls and roll in coconut.

DRIED PEAR AND PINEAPPLE

Peel pears, cut in half and scoop out seeds and core. Dip in heavy syrup and drain. Fill cavity with drained crushed pineapple and dry. This makes a most delicious confection.

REHYDRATION OF FRUITS

When fruits are going to be stewed, soak first to shorten cooking time. They may be simmered without soaking. Home dried fruits will have more moisture removed than commercially dried fruits and will be harder. To soften fruit before eating as a snack, put an assortment in a bottle. Pour water on and off once. Tighten lid and let stand overnight.

Soften fruits before using in breads or cookies and baby food. Soften fruit Leather in hot water.

PREPARATION OF VEGETABLES FOR DEHYDRATION

You should select fresh vegetables at the peak of their maturity and dry immediately after harvest for best results. ANY vegetable can be dried. With a preliminary steam or hot dip you can obtain a satisfactory product. Some fruits and vegetables tend to lose flavor and color if stored too long. Wash all fresh produce thoroughly and cut or slice evenly.

BLANCHING

Blanching consists of precooking vegetables over steam. This process will inactivate or destroy the enzymes responsible for undesirable color changes, odor and texture. It also facilitates quick dehydration and rehydration of vegetables. If this process is omitted, some vegetables will be tough and faded in color.

The exceptions for blanching are the seasoning vegetables, such as celery, tomatoes, garlic, onions, and peppers. The latter three will have a stronger flavor if unblanched.

Potatoes can be blanched over steam until translucent. This is easier than boiling and preserves more of the minerals.

HOW

1. Use a kettle having a close fitting lid and a wire basket or strainer placed in the kettle so that the steam will circulate freely around the vegetables.

2. Have the water boiling briskly before putting the prepared vegetable into the kettle.

3. Have a layer of vegetables in the steamer not more than 3" deep.

4. Steam the vegetables until hot through - in the case of leafy vegetables - until they wilt. Sliced potatoes should be put right in boiling water for 3-4 minutes.

5. Remove vegetables from steam and dip in cold water before placing on trays to dry - in your dehydrator.

TIME PERIOD FOR BLANCHING AND DRYING

PRODUCT	SIZE	BLANCHING TIME	DRYING TIME
Asparagus	Any length	5 minutes	6-8 hours
Beets (cooked)	Sliced 1/4"	5 minutes	5-8 hours
Beans – green	2" lengths	5 minutes	8-10 hours
Beans – green	French cut	2 minutes	6-7 hours
Broccoli	3" lengths	5 minutes	5-6 hours
Carrots	Sliced or cubed	5 minutes	6-7 hours
Cabbage	Shredded	2 minutes	4-5 hours
Cauliflower	Pieces	5 minutes	6-8 hours
Corn	Kernels	5 minutes	6-8 hours
Celery	1/2" pieces	2 minutes	8-10 hours
Mushrooms	Sliced	none	12-14 hours
Eggplant	1/4" slices	3 minutes	6-7 hours
Okra	¼" lengths	5 minutes	6-8 hours
Parsnips	Sliced	5 minutes	6-8 hours

*Place on nylon net covered trays.

CORN

4 qts. corn
½ cup sugar or desired sweetening

1 cup canned evaporated milk
4 tsp. salt

Mix. Pour into two shallow pans and bake in oven at 350 for 45 min. Drain and place on nylon net covered trays.

REHYDRATION OF VEGETABLES

Vegetables to be eaten raw should be soaked in cold water in the refrigerator until all the water is back in. Vegetables to be cooked can be soaked in hot water. 1½ cups of water to 1 cup vegetables, before cooking.

DEHYDRATING OF GREENS AND HERBS

PRODUCT	PREPARATION	BLANCHING	APPX. DRYING TIME
Beet greens	Wash-use leafy part	2 minutes	1-2 hours
Celery tops	Wash-lay on trays	none	1-2 hours
Chives	Wash-lay on trays	none	1-2 hours
Chard	Wash-lay on trays	2 minutes	2 hours
Comfrey	Wash-use before plant blooms	none	1-2 hours
Dandelion greens	Wash-use leaves	none	1-2 hours
Dandelion root	Wash-spread out	none	2-4 hours
Kale	Wash-spread out	2 minutes	2-4 hours
Lettuce	Wash-spread out	none	1 hour
Mint	Wash-spread out	none	1 hour
Parsley	Wash-spread out	none	1 hour
Raspberry leaves	Wash-spread out	none	1 hour
Sage	Wash-spread out	none	1 hour

Any other herbs can be dried the same as above, You will note that any herbs or greens will stay green when dried in a dehydrator, They fade when dried in the sun.

STORAGE OF VEGETABLES AND HERBS
When herbs are dry, pull leaves off stems and crush - store in bottles with tight lids. Vegetables should be completely dry before storing, same as for fruits in a dark and cool place, If you don't have a dark place, wrap the bottles with newspaper, Check both fruits and vegetables once a month for mold, If mold has developed, wash or scrape off and dry more thoroughly, You must keep moisture out.

RECIPES FOR DEHYDRATED VEGETABLES

VEGETABLES FOR SOUP - DRY VEGETABLES SEPARATELY THEN COMBINE AN ASSORTMENT FOR SOUP OR STEW AND STORE THEM IN PLASTIC ZIP LOCK BAGS,

Carrots - 45%
Onions - 21 %
Green Peppers - 8%
Cabbage - 12%
Tomatoes - (optional)

VEGETABLE BROTH
Carrots
Celery
Onions
Parsley
Spinach

Grind or blend into a powder, Combine powder with tomato juice, season, and simmer, strain if necessary, Add a bouillon cube either beef or chicken for variety,

TOMATO POWDER

Dehydrated tomatoes ground into a flour make a very concentrated product for tomato paste, juice, Catsup, etc, This powder can be added directly to soups, spaghetti, pizzas, etc, KEEP SEALED IN AIR TIGHT CONTAINERS,

Any vegetable can be made into a powder for various uses - made into instant soup, added to breads, mixed into spreads and dips. Boiling water added to vegetable powder makes instant baby food. Backpackers, hunters, fishermen, astronauts, and just plain people will appreciate this beef stew and chili sauce leather. Eat it dry or rehydrate it.

CHILI SAUCE LEATHER

1 quart peeled, cut up tomatoes
¼ cup sugar or honey
2 medium onions, cut up
¼ tsp cinnamon
1 green pepper, cut up

1 tsp allspice
1 tsp salt
1/8 tsp cloves
¼ cup vinegar
Dash red pepper

Puree in blender and spread thinly on plastic wrap on cookie sheet. Dehydrate.

VEGETABLE BEEF STEW LEATHER

2 ½ lbs. ground beef, lightly browned
Cook the following until tender in a small amount of water:

4 large potatoes
1 green pepper
3 large carrots
4 stalks celery
2 medium onions

1/2 bunch parsley
Blend vegetables and meat.
Season with:
1 envelope Lipton Onion Soup Mix

Salt and pepper to taste. Spread ¼ inch thick on oiled cookie sheets or plastic wrap. You may also use your own favorite stew recipe and blend the same way. Dry.

ZUCCHINI CHIPS

Large zucchini, peeled and sliced thin. Blanch 2 minutes.
Spread out on trays. Salt - dry until crisp. USE AS CRACKERS OR CHIPS.

ZUCCHINI CASSEROLE

3-4 cups rehydrated zucchini
Cook about 10 minutes in small amount of water. Place in 2 qt. casserole.
2 cups white sauce to which has been added:
1 tsp worcestershire sauce
2 tbsp minced onion
1 cup cubed cheese (add last)
Pour sauce over zucchini and top with buttered bread crumbs.
Bake 30 minutes at 350°.

CORN AND SUMMER SQUASH
(MEXICAN STYLE)

Rehydrate vegetables before measuring

2 tbsp butter
3 cups corn (cooked until tender)
3 cups sliced tomatoes
2 cups sliced summer squash

3 tbsp minced onions
2 tsp salt
1/8 tsp pepper

Melt butter in skillet - add vegetables and seasonings. Cook 10-15 minutes.

GLAZED CARROTS

3 cups rehydrated carrots.
Cook until tender. Drain.
Add 1/4 cup orange juice.

1 tbsp cornstarch
2 tbsp butter

Cook until carrots are glazed.

POTATO AU GRATIN

Rehydrate sliced or cubed potatoes and boil until tender. Place in baking dish.

Sauce:

1/4 cup butter or oil
1/2 cup chopped onions
3/8 cup flour

1/2 tsp salt
1 tbsp dry parsley
1/2 pound medium sharp cheese

Heat oil, add onion and saute. Add flour, salt and milk and cook until smooth. Cut half cheese in cubes and add to sauce. Pour over potatoes and cover with remaining cheese (grated). Bake at 350° for about 45 minutes.

CORN BEEF CHIPS

1 can corn beef
3 cups cooked potatoes
1/2 cup chopped onions

1/2 tsp salt
1 tsp prepared mustard

Blend, adding enough potato water to get an action going. Spread out on the trays and dehydrate. (optional) Cut circles with an opened NO.2 size can and store in same. Excellent for back packers.

CORN CHIPS

2 cups corn (cooked)
4 oz sharp cheese
2 tsp garlic salt

1 tsp onion salt
1/2 cup water
1/2 cup wheat flour

Blend and spread out on two plastic wrap covered trays. Dry until set. Score in squares and finish drying until crisp. Takes about 4-5 hours drying time.

YAMS AND APPLES

Rehydrate yams and apples. Alternate layers of yams and apples in casserole and pour sauce over all.

Sauce:

1/2 cup sugar or honey
2 tbsp cornstarch
1/4 cup butter

2 tsp lemon juice
2 cups fruit juice – apricot, pineapple, and orange are a good combination

Cook until clear. Bake until hot through.

DEHYDRATION OF MEATS AND FISH JERKY

To make Jerky, remove fat from cheap cuts of beef shank, chuck, or venison. Partially freeze for easier slicing. Cut in strip 1/4" thick 1" wide. Cutting along and not across the grain. Pound into the meat a seasoning of salt, pepper, oregano, marjoram, basil and thyme. Spread on trays of dehydrator and dry until it will snap. Takes from 5-7 hours.

Variation: From your meat man buy beef meat marinade and mix with water as directed on package, omitting oil. Mix 1 tbsp, liquid smoke into 1 cup marinade. Marinate meat strips in mixture from 3 hrs to 2 days in refrigerator. For venison add garlic, onion powder and soy sauce.

HAMBURGER JERKY
(SUBMITTED BY ALTA GARRETT)

1 lb. very lean ground beef
1pkg. beef gravy mix
1/4 cup soy sauce
3 tbsp. catsup

2 or 3 tsp. liquid smoke
1 tsp. onion salt
1/2 tsp. garlic salt
1 rounded tbsp. brown sugar

Mix well and spread out on plastic covered trays. Dry at 150° for 2 hours Remove and score in 1" wide strips. Finish drying until firm & chewy - about 3 hrs. Jerky made from regular hamburger should be stored in refrigerator as fat in meat will go rancid.

HAM OR BEEF T.V.P. JERKY
(ALTA GARRETT)

2 cups ham or beef T.V.P. (textured vegetable protein). 4 cups warm water - Let stand 3 hrs. Blend until smooth.

Add:

1/4 cup soy sauce
2 tbsp. brown sugar
1/3 worcestershire sauce
3-4 tbsp. powdered onion

1 tbsp. powdered tomato
3 to 4 tbsp. - liquid smoke
1/2 tsp. garlic salt
1 tbsp. salt

Mix well and spread evenly on 2 plastic covered dehydrator trays. Set temperature at 150°. Check in 3 hours to see if Jerky can be turned and cut into strips. Dry 2 to 3 more hours or until chewy.

RABBIT, TURKEY, OR CHICKEN (LEFTOVER)

Always trim fat off first then cut into slices 1/4" thick. Place on tray and dehydrate. This is good as a snack or in recipes.

FISH

Fillet fish and cut in strips 3/4" thick - Soak in brine (1/4 cup salt to 1 qt. water) for 1 hour. Remove, blot, sprinkle with salt and pepper. Brush with barbeque sauce to which 1 tbsp. of liquid smoke has been added. Place on trays and dry at 150° until surfaces are dry. Skin will peel off very easily after fish is dry.

OTHER USES

Those people who are leaning toward raw foods will discover that many foods can be dehydrated instead of baked, thereby preserving precious nutrients. Your dehydrator can double as a yogurt maker, crouton, bread crumb, nut, noodle, and granola drier.

Contributions

Leathers can be made from leftovers such as sour cream enchiladas, beef chow mein, pork chops and tomato sauce, or any main dish. Blend and spread on Saran Wrap to dry. These make tasty trail snacks for the back packer or for hungry children.

- Lynda Laughlin, Green River, Wyoming

Dried Fruit Combo - Mixture of dried apples, cherries, pineapple, bananas, peaches, fruit leather squares, puffed wheat and puffed or parched corn, sunflower seeds, nuts of any kind. (Purchase puffed corn at a health food store.)

- Violet Squires, Centerville, Utah

Nuts -Dry about 4 hours or until nut is too hard to pierce with finger nail. Seal in clean jars with new lids by placing in 200° oven for 45 minutes.

- Barbara Huish, Chandler, Arizona

Eggs -Slightly beat eggs and spread out on Saran Wrap. Dehydrate at 1350 until leathery. powder in blender.

- Marie English, Salt Lake City, Utah

For berry Leather-Combine any berry mixed half and half with apple sauce.
Orange Peel-Soak strips of orange peel in honey for 2 or 3 days. Drain and dry at low heat. Delicious as a snack or for flavoring.

- Mary Lundskog, Murray, Utah

Dried Flowers -Preserve flowers in silica gel in the dehydrator set at 1600. A rose takes four hours to dry versus the usual four days.

- Joy Catmull, Hunter, Utah

HONEY
"Bee Prepared" by Arthur W. Andersen

THE PERFECT FOOD

Raw honey contains proteins, carbohydrates, hormones, organic acids, and antimicrobial compounds. Honey is a good carbohydrate source and supplies energy at 63 calories per tablespoon. It also contains a rich supply of live enzymes, which are required for the proper functioning of all body systems.

Honey is more than just merely a sweetener. It is a storehouse of essential vitamins, minerals and trace elements. It contains Vitamins A, C, D, E, K, and Beta carotene, and almost all vitamins of the B-complex, which are needed in the system for the digestion and metabolism of sugar. The vitamin C content varies considerably, depending on the source of the nectar. Some kinds may contain as much as 300 milligrams of vitamin C per 100 grams of honey. The mineral rich honey has calcium, phosphorus, magnesium, potassium, silicon, sulfur, copper, manganese, sodium, chlorine, iodine and iron.

A NATURAL ENERGIZER

From the beginning of time honey has been used to supply energy and to rejuvenate the body. Athletes from all over the world use honey to increase their reserve of immediate energy, which is due to its balanced sugar formula. Honey needs no intermediate steps for proper digestion, and because of this it is a source of rapidly supplied energy. The glycogen in one spoon of honey is known to pass into the bloodstream in 10 minutes to produce quick energy. When taken with a calcium supplement, the glucose in honey can increase the body's uptake of the mineral by nearly 25 percent.

HEALING PROPERTIES

Honey has many Healing Properties. It is known to promote the rapid healing of wounds. It is perfect for any kind of injury which involves breaking the skin. It protects against infection while boosting the healing process. . Research has confirmed that honey does indeed exert antibacterial action on certain pathogens which cause diarrhea. It is an anti-allergenic, anti-inflammatory, a bactericidal and expectorant that insures the body's defense and gives it the capacity to regenerate its attacked cells. Honey has been found to help in chronic bronchitis, asthmatic bronchitis, bronchial asthma, chronic rhinitis, allergic rhinitis and sinusitis. This simple, efficient, cheap and with not side effects deserves to be better known and integrated within common antiseptics.

Note: Honey should never be used to treat any condition if a sensitivity to honey exists. Anyone who is, should establish whether they are allergic to honey before using it therapeutically.

WHEAT
"The Amazing Wheat Book" by LeArta A. Moulton

THE STAFF OF LIFE

"Man cannot live by bread alone," the Bible says. But whole grain is surely a good start. Ironically, even though refined "white" flour became popular as a symbol of wealth, the whole wheat kernel is far more complete nutritionally. We still do not know which constituents alone or together create the good effect of the whole wheat grain, but, we do know men and women who eat more whole grains live longer. Research has shown that eating whole grains is associated with lower risk of deaths, and heart disease. Other studies show that eating whole grains improves blood pressure and blood sugar levels in the short term, reducing risk of heart disease, stroke and diabetes. Regular use of whole grain is important in building a digestive tolerance for roughage.

In Western countries most people eat less than one serving of whole grain daily, compared with several of white flour. "Public health problems arising from inactivity and poor dietary habits will be a great challenge for decades to come

Note: Nearly all the vitamins are milled out of white flour and only B1, B2 and niacin are returned to "Enriched Flour."

NUTRITIONAL VALUE

Nutrients in the whole wheat are pantothenic acid, folic acid, biotin, cholin, inisitol, Vitamins B1, B2, B6 and E. The minerals are iron, cobalt, potassium, magnesium, zinc, copper and molybdenum. In order to retain all these nutrients, the whole wheat must be used as soon after grinding as possible, or stored in a freezer.

The bran or outer covering is made up of 4 layers rich in minerals, protein and vitamin B. The part that sprouts (the germ) contains a rich amount of vitamin B complex, vitamin E, protein, fat and mineral matter. Together the Bran and Germ contain organic phosphates which provide food for the brain and nerve cells. The endosperm or main bulk of the kernel contains no vitamins and very few minerals (this is what the white four mostly consists of and was perhaps only intended to provide food for the germ to sprout.

HOW TO BUY AND STORE

Fort the average consumption of bread and cereal, one years supply should ne about 70 pounds for a child and 300 lbs. for an adult. Choose a hard winter wheat or hard spring wheat with a grad #2 or better. Look for a high protein content of 16% or above. It should be cleaned but unwashed.

Wheat can be stored in tin, plastic or glass containers. It should be stored in a cool dry place. Never place metal on cement or dirt floor. Set containers on a wooden slat or shelves to prevent condensation and moisture. Containers should be clean and free of odors and able to affect a tight seal to keep out insects and moisture.

NOTES:

NOTES:

INDEX